W9-CEN-069

DISCARD

cop. 1
NOV 7 1984

FORM 125 M

The Chicago Public Library
BUSINESS/SCIENCE/TECHNOLOGY DIVISION
THE CHICAGO PUBLIC LIBRARY

Received

FORM 19

BACKUS STRIKES BACK

BACKUS STRIKES BACK

Jim Backus and **Henny Backus**

Foreword by George Burns

STEIN AND DAY/*Publishers*/New York

Photograph credits: Jim Backus on "Person to Person," © CBS, Inc., 1984, used by permission. Mr. Magoo © UPA Pictures, Inc., used by permission. Jim and Henny Backus and Tony Curtis from the MGM release *Don't Make Waves,* © 1967 Metro-Goldwyn-Mayer Inc., reprinted by permission. Jim and Henny Backus and Ralph Edwards on "This Is Your Life," courtesy Ralph Edwards Productions, used by permission. Jim and Henny Backus, Jack Lescoulie, Charles Van Doren, and Betty Hargrove on the "Today" show, used by permission. Jim and Henny Backus, courtesy Doré Records, used by permission. Jim's act and Jim and his furry friend, courtesy Freemont Hotel, Las Vegas, used by permission. Jim and Tybee Brascia, courtesy Robert Landau, used by permission. Jim Backus on the "Mike Douglas Show," © 1979 Michael Leshnov, used by permission. Photos by Nate Cutler used by permission.

Portions of the song "Ac-cent-tchu-ate the Positive" by Johnny Mercer and Harold Arlen, © 1944 Harwin Music Co., © renewed 1972 Harwin Music Co. International Copyright Secured. All Rights Reserved. Used By Permission.

First published in 1984
Copyright © 1984 by Jim and Henny Backus
All rights reserved, Stein and Day, Incorporated
Designed by Terese B. Platten
Printed in the United States of America
STEIN AND DAY/ *Publishers*
Scarborough House
Briarcliff Manor, N.Y. 10510

RC
386.2
.B33
1984

Library of Congress Cataloging in Publication Data

Backus, Jim.
  Backus strikes back.

  1. Backus, Jim.   2. Basal ganglia—Diseases—Patients
—California—Biography.   3. Actors—California—Biography.
4. Diagnostic errors.   I. Backus, Henny.   II. Title.
RC386.2.B33   1984   362.1'9683   [B]   83-40357
ISBN 0-8128-2962-X

To
Frances Franco,
Patsy de Shields,
Harriet Bergere,
Nancy Brock,
and
Kathy Segal,
whose flying fingers through the years made our
words visible.
To
Linda Palmer, who made this book possible.
And to
our dearest George!

CONTENTS

FOREWORD

I recently got a letter from my good friends Jim and Henny Backus asking me to write a foreword for this book. I didn't read the book, but I did read the letter.

I've written four books, which is pretty good for a guy who only read two, but I've never written a foreword before. So this is going to be my first foreword. I'm very excited—I couldn't sleep last night.

I did a lot of research on forewords, and the trick of a good foreword is that it shouldn't be too long a foreword or too short a foreword. Another thing, it shouldn't be too good a foreword, or it'll make the book look bad. So you see, a good foreword by me would be a bad foreword for Jim and Henny. Incidentally, if you've forgotten who Jim and Henny are, they're the ones who wrote this book. And if you've forgotten who I am, I'm the one writing this foreword.

It's not easy to sit down and try to write a bad foreword. I don't know how so many people have managed to do it.

I just read this foreword over, and I'd better stop. It's beginning to sound good.

George Burns
(Author of Foreword)

By the way, I lied. I read the book and loved it. It's a very touching and funny book. It made me cry, and it made me laugh, and it made me buy a dictionary. It's a very good dictionary, but it has a bad foreword. Henny and Jim, I love you.

PREFACE

This is the story of a disease and how it affected me.

To say I was not influenced or, to put it mildly, inspired by Norman Cousins's book, would be a blatant understatement. His is a sensitive, carefully documented account by an extremely gifted and erudite man. Mine is simply the way it happened to me, from my side of the desk.

I did no research. I want to present what I gleaned as a layman. If some of my statements are erroneous, my apologies to the AMA. There are some policies of theirs that I don't see eye to eye with, either.

I did not use the actual names of any of the doctors or medical facilities. I thought it better that way.

Most of the doctors I encountered, I found to be dedicated, gifted, concerned human beings, individually. Collectively? Well, let any hotel announce that they are catering a medical dinner, and 90 percent of the waiters will phone in sick. Doctors are right under airline captains and slightly above baseball players in line to get a Mickey Finn.

I wonder what they think of us?

I want to thank Henny for picking up her pen and for putting mine back in my fingers.

BACKUS STRIKES BACK

1

Evaluation

"WELL, IT LOOKS like it might be Parkinson's disease."

The young doctor looked at me standing there in my shorts. I looked back, feeling for all the world like a plucked chicken. That couldn't be me he was talking about, could it?

"He's got every symptom," concurred his colleague, an equally young neurologist stroking his cavalry officer's mustache, which he hoped would give his opinion quiet authority.

Both were wearing three-quarter length, beautifully tailored, white clinic coats that served to accentuate their slightly flared slacks and matching Gucci loafers. I could hear the expensive rattle of their jewelry carefully concealed under their Battaglia shirts. They were wearing more chains than Kunta Kinte.

I struggled to get into my trousers and had difficulty keeping my balance.

This did not go unnoticed by one of the young healers, who quickly made a note on his Earl Scheib clipboard.*

---

*Earl Scheib: A friendly man who advertizes extensively in the Los Angeles papers. He offers to paint your car for ridiculously low credit terms. All free estimates are made by a fierce-looking man carrying huge clipboards.

I grappled awkwardly with one of my shoes. This, too, was noted. Their scrutiny made the heretofore simple task all the more arduous.

No wonder I'm staggering, I rationalized, after an hour of poking and prodding, not to mention jumping on one foot and then the other—and that business of touching my nose with my forefinger. Why hadn't Rick, my trusted internist and friend, sent me to a real doctor? To me, a real doctor is a kindly old curmudgeon with a stethoscope around his neck and that ever-present little black bag at his side.

"Mr. Backus . . ."

I was having difficulty buttoning my shirt.

"We're going to call Rick and tell him what we found. Understand you'll be seeing him later this afternoon."

I almost garroted myself tying my tie as the synergistic duo left. Boy, would Rick hear from me—wasting a whole morning with these clowns!

Assembling myself as best I could, I angrily stumbled across the waiting room, almost tripping on the rug. A voice halted me.

"Good-bye, Mr. Backus. Could I validate your parking ticket?" The voice came from an attractive plastic nurse, carefully starched and siliconed. I handed her my ticket.

"Oh, I see you're not in the sports car section," she laughed, her little red tongue darting out to dampen the validation stamp. "Have a nice day," she tinkled.

As I left, the understated Muzak segued into "I've Got a Feeling I'm Falling." Now this I could relate to.

Later that afternoon, I was seated in Rick's office. I sat there and looked at him. He hadn't changed much. He was tall, still slim, with crinkly blue eyes, and, even now, there was still a bit of red in his gray hair. He had finished with the amenities.

"Sally, no phone calls. I'll be with Mr. Backus."

The whole thing had the unreality of a badly staged play. I couldn't get comfortable for some reason, and I was exhausted. I guess it was the trip through the indoor-parking facilities of Rick's building. That was always unnerving. Up the badly marked ramps, through the tunnel of the winds, over the cantilevered catwalk, and finally into the medical complex itself—a beehive of orthodontists, urologists, cardiologists, radiologists, orthopedists, and, of course, the proctologists who were, naturally, housed on the bottom floor.

The lobby was done in early Wayne Newton, with everything short of slot machines, rather like a Las Vegas casino with a hysterectomy. It was dominated by a garishly lit drugstore, resplendent with stuffed pandas and giant Barbie dolls that went pee pee and ca ca. At the center counter was the friendly druggist busily dispensing Valiums, and over on the corner shelf was a "special" on do-it-yourself blood pressure kits and designer bed pans. God forbid you should get sick in this medical building.

I remembered for one fleeting moment the wonderful office Rick used to have. It was in a lovely two-story building with a real outdoor parking lot located on winding Sunset Boulevard, just before it made its final dip to the sea. No super highways, no Manchester off-ramp, no Centinela exit; no airport bypass. (One false turn and you'd be sucked up by a jumbo jet bound for New York.)

I was startled out of my reverie.

"Well, Jim, it's time we had a talk. I heard from Dr. Korman and Dr. Romaine, and . . ."

"Oh, you mean the Frick and Frack of the neurology circuit?"

Rick smiled tolerantly. "Frick and Frack, as you call them, are not two of the most conservative members of our profession. But Jim, believe me, they're damned good doctors. I checked them out. And remember, Jim, they were your choice."

"Well, we had the same agent," I replied weakly. "Them . . . me . . . the astronauts."

A drop of flop sweat fell in a straight line right into my shoe like an icy bullet.

"They said something about Parkinson's disease or something," I volunteered weakly.

Rick nodded.

The muted noise of the traffic seven floors below seeped its way through the sealed windows. I remembered Rick's old office, where you could hear kids playing in the street and, so help me, occasionally, an organ grinder.

For a shocked moment, everything stood still. I looked out the window. The scene is indelibly etched in my mind. The scrofulous palm trees piercing their way up through the yellow smog, the pale, orange sun sinking behind the wrinkled mountains.

Parkinson's disease? I'd heard of that.

I always confused it with those other two diseases. Never could sort them out.

Christ! Hadn't I emceed a telethon for Parkinson's? Or was it muscular dystrophy? Wasn't it in Amarillo, Texas? What difference. Platoons of pathetic patients in wheelchairs . . . human pretzels.

Hell, these were things that happened to someone else!

"You're sure?" I asked Rick.

"As sure as you can be about anything," my doctor told me compassionately. "With this disease, there is no diagnosis, merely an evaluation. The last time you were in, you told me you were afraid to play golf. You couldn't make the shoulder turn. You were dizzy . . . lost your balance."

"Yeah, I used to be good. Now I play golf like old people fuck."

He ignored my down-home simile. "You said you had difficulty swimming. You had trouble coordinating your arms and legs. Couldn't shave . . . tie your tie . . . write . . . handle a fork." He consulted his folder. "And you were taking little shuffling steps. I was suspicious, but I wanted to be sure. So we did that brain scan. Nothing was wrong there, but . . ."

"It scared the shit out of me. Shoving my head in that fireless cooker. And now it's Frick and Frack. And their evaluation is what we'll have to go along with, right?"

There was a heavy pause. An elevator door clanged somewhere.

"Well, what do we do, Rick? You're the doctor."

It felt like we were playing a terrible scene, and soon, hopefully, someone would yell "Cut!"

"Look, Jim, that's enough for today. We'll outline a program for you. Remember, with this disease, if you follow a rigid regimen, it can be arrested. Not cured," he emphasized, "but arrested. That is, if you exercise, exercise, exercise, and take your medication."

"Medication?"

"We won't go into it now, Jimmy. You've had a rough day, and the weekend's ahead of you. But on Monday, we'll start you on a drug that's been very effective: L-Dopa."

"L-Dopa? Sounds like something you get in a cigar store in Tijuana. Guaranteed to cure the clap."

Rick laughed because it was the merciful thing to do. He rose from his chair. "Don't worry, Jim. You'll feel better on Monday when we start your drugs and therapy."

We walked to the door. Rick clasped my hand. Thirty years of love in that handshake. The door closed behind me. I made my way down the hall into the elevator, over the cantilevered catwalk, through the tunnel of the winds, down the dimly lit ramps, past the sign that read "Parking for the Handicapped."

On the way home, I had a chance to review the bidding. Somehow, the drive had an air of finality about it. Every familiar landmark I passed I seemed to be seeing for the first time. The traffic was heavy, and, as we inched along Wilshire Boulevard, I studied the drivers alongside. They were all in shirt-sleeves, their polyester coats draped carefully over the passenger seat. Why were they all so young . . . so healthy!

My own thoughts drew me inward. In a way, I was relieved. At least now I knew what was wrong with me.

For the past three years things had been wrong. I tried to keep them hidden, even from Henny. The dizziness, the baby steps, the loss of balance.

Rick had examined me many times during those three years. Nothing had shown up. Every time I missed a step, I panicked and phoned him. I didn't know what else to do. My "cry wolf" calls must have been a prime pain in the ass.

Then the tests started. Nothing!

Meantime, I was working. Movies, television appearances, talk shows, two thousand radio commercials. How did I do it? A nightmare. Hanging on by my fingernails, nerves stretched to the breaking point. "This one's for the Gipper!" What was wrong with me?

Jogging! That would do it—the newest wonder drug. First the Adidas running shoes, then the jogging suit from Saks, the stopwatch, the big earphones with the built-in transistors to keep me abreast of the news.

I staked out a course around our yard. (That's what we called it in Cleveland. Here in Bel-Air, it's the garden.) Okay. So I ran around the garden—twenty-five times, which equalled one mile. I did it every day.

I have heard that running creates a sense of euphoria, a "high" unequaled by booze, pot, or cocaine. Bullshit! It was sheer drudgery. Each step was a nightmare. I hated every bush I passed. But I did it, damn it! It would make me well.

Somewhere along the line, I picked up a psychiatrist-analyst-shrink, whatever. I can't even remember his name now. I must admit this analyst tried and tried, but to no avail. Every session was its own crisis.

"I'm starting a picture Tuesday. What'll I do?"

"Take two Valiums."

Sure, why not? And if they wear off, I'll just take two more.

I learned to do it deftly, even while the cameras were rolling. All in one swift, sneaky, little move—no Parkinsonisms there!

I turned into the Bel-Air gate and then into my own driveway.

Henny must have talked to Rick. She was standing in the doorway, holding a tall, frosted glass.

God, she was pretty, and I love her so!

2

The Tapes

THIS IS HENNY

I HAD TRIED my best to cheer Jim up. I had even served him his favorite Cleveland dinner: shrimp cocktail, roast leg of lamb with mint jelly, mashed potatoes with gravy, and apple pie a la mode. I tried my damndest to pull him out of it, but the presence of Dr. Parkinson, our uninvited guest, was not to be dispelled.

Later, in bed, we watched Johnny Carson, laughing perfunctorily at his irreverent monologue. I finally switched off the light and kissed Jim good night. It was a special, tender kiss, one I would always remember.

THIS IS JIM

I lay back, and a kaleidoscope of Henny memories flashed before my closed eyes. Not fantasies—these were replays of the real thing, edited by time.

It was as though I were playing a tape.

Our first date at the Algonquin.

Getting married twice in one week—once for her family, in Philadelphia, and then again for mine, in Cleveland. No wonder it's a success. Ours is the only marriage I know of that had an out-of-town tryout.

Our first trip to Rome. There is a story Henny tells on herself. This is the way she tells it:

I was upstairs getting dressed for dinner. Jim was in the lobby, entirely surrounded by lady tourists in their mink stoles and orchids who were getting autographs for their kids. As he was handing back a pencil, a hand with long, sharp, very red nails reached into the crowd and pushed, pulled, and propelled him back of a post behind a potted palm. This lady was the antithesis of the lady tourists. She was wearing a micro-mini skirt, mesh hose, and shoes with stiletto heels. Her eyelashes swept the floor.

Jim was at a loss, so he meekly asked, "Would you like my autograph?"

"Oooo," she purred through half-closed eyes, "I woulda lika you autographa on a Banka America Expressa card."

Still at a loss, he said, "I don't get it!"

So she made sure he did. "You getta eet, babee," she breathed as she undulated her hips insinuatingly. "You coma weeth me, and you getta eet! Joost geeve me one hundred Americano dollars."

Well! Jim's been around, and he knew the best way to get rid of her was to insult her, so he said, "One hundred dollars? I'll give you five!"

It worked. She did what we in show business call a "rave off." She hissed and spat and made the sign of the horns at him. Then she called down curses that went back to Romulus and Remus and stamped out of the lobby and into the night.

About fifteen minutes later, Jim and I were having a predinner drink in the hotel bar when this same lady, still on the prowl, stuck her head in the door and cased the room. She spotted us and stalked over to our table. Then, pointing her finger at me, she cried in a voice of thunder, "See! She whatta you get for five dollars!"

The tape clicked off.

I looked over at Henny—wife, concubine, and full-time enigma. I sensed she was praying. She segued into a gentle purr. That night sleep came unwillingly, dragging its flannel feet.

I shut my eyes, but the tapes rolled on.

These were doctor tapes. New ones, from this afternoon. The two Whiz Kids, Korman and Romaine, with their "now" wardrobe and, as Rick had said, an infallible knowledge of their craft. Then the hour with

Rick. Rick with his kindness, his empathy, his almost spiritual approach to medicine. Thirty years of Rick tapes, mostly biyearly checkups, all with the usual expected happy endings.

"Everything seems to be in order, Jim. Wish you'd stop smoking and cut down on the booze. You've got the heart of an eighteen-year-old boy."

"And he wants it back!" I added with a Groucho Marx leer. Our biannual joke.

The handshake and shoulder clasp. High emotion for two Wasps. Down the hall, Dr. Gambini was soul-kissing his patients out the door.

Montages began to form behind my tightly shut eyes. Vivid and close. People unable to move or speak, hideously crippled. They flashed one after the other. They beckoned to me, these "Parkys," as I had once heard them called. I tried to turn them off, but I couldn't. I had no control over them. I lay there, cold and wet.

Finally they turned grainy and black and white, like a silent movie, and I saw him clearly—the old family doctor we had when I was a kid. I'll break a ground rule and tell you his real name. A name far better than any team of writers for "Love Boat" or even "Fantasy Island" could conjure up. Dr. Laurence A. Pomeroy! Now *that* was a name for a doctor. He stood there with that stethoscope around his neck, his little black bag at his side, and smiled at me. He looked like a cross between Douglas Fairbanks, Sr., and Lewis Stone. I always suspected my mother had a sneaker for the old croaker (a euphemism employed by my father). I remember when Dr. Laurence A. Pomeroy condemned me to an emergency appendectomy. He drove me to the hospital himself, in his Buick. A Cadillac would have been ostentatious and anything less would indicate he wasn't doing all that well. A far cry from Drs. Romaine and Korman with their matching DeLoreans and their ring-a-ding-ding license plates.

I kept the tapes rolling. Doctors I had known in foreign lands, anything but the memories of this terrible afternoon.

(CLICK)

A German doctor in Italy who I'm sure had been left behind by a retreating Wehrmacht. He had injected the virus-ridden cast of our picture with his own devil's brew. Later, a critic commented that our film had "a dreamlike quality."

More doctor tapes.

Across the channel to England. Ellstree Studios. My temperature, 102°. A country doctor summoned to the studio from just having helped a mare foal. He wore country-squire puttees and knickers. His prescription—unlimited brandy from the commissary. Since actors in England are limited to two drinks at lunch, I became the prize guest at Ellstree, me and my prescription. The English firmly believe that spirits have the same magical power we Americans know that chicken soup has.
   (CLICK)

England again. The staid London Clinic. Having a high colonic or "proper wash" (another English cure-all), administered by "our Mrs. Boyle," an ancient, five-foot-tall technician whose long gray hair kept caressing my buttocks, and who seemed far more interested in the whereabouts of Tab Hunter than her hose.
   (CLICK OFF)

A few days after the diagnosis, I was flown up to San Francisco and checked into a hospital. After admittance and just after they manacled me into that celluloid bracelet that even the great Harry Houdini couldn't escape from (but somehow *I* did), I remembered something. The incident of the bracelet reminded me that a few years before, I had been in St. John's Hospital for minor surgery—a Roto-Rooter* job, up the picturesque urinary canal.
   Three days later, aside from voiding Nixonbuttons, I was feeling fine and sitting up when it hit me! I was due *this* afternoon at the insurance doctor's office to be examined for a movie I was starting the following week. (Before you begin working on a picture or TV series, the producer insures you so that *he's* protected; then, in case anything happens to you, like a collapse, a stroke, or a coronary, he's covered. Hence the examination, and you'd *just better pass it!*)
   So there I was at 1:00 P.M., sitting up in a hospital bed in Santa Monica and due in a doctor's office in Hollywood at 2:00! To this day, I don't know how I coerced the nurse into letting me have my clothes, but I did! So far so good. But what about cab fare? Ever borrow $20.00 from a nun? Well, just don't get in the habit!

---

*Roto-Rooter: A voracious-looking, dull instrument used for cleaning out clogged latrines and/or sewers. Also great for parties. V., to roto-root; to give pleasure.

Half an hour later, I was calmly sitting in the doctor's waiting room filling out an insurance form prior to the medical examination itself:

Any insanity in your family .... No
Any diseases of the heart,
    lungs, liver in the past year .... No
Have you been hospitalized in
    the last six months .... No.

No? I glanced down, and there it was! That telltale hospital I.D. bracelet. How I got it off my wrist, I'll never know. I had to do something, and quickly. Would you believe that I had a fairly complete physical examination, and the doctor never discovered where I had craftily hidden my bracelet? Thank God, he wasn't a proctologist!

This San Francisco hospital had put me into their pride-and-joy: "The Golden Gate Room," so-called because of its imposing view of the San Francisco harbor. Imagine being in a hospital bed and having to look at all that! And, what's more, atop a nearby building, a party was in progress. I could make out the people mingling on the terrace. I could hear the background music and the tinkling of the glasses. Better a room overlooking an air shaft.

I pressed a button and my bed swiveled upward under my knees. Hospital beds are supposed to be super comfortable. I pressed another button. The bed shifted. Somehow I could not make myself snug. Then I remembered. One of the symptoms of my disease is the inability to get comfortable, even if lying on Dolly Parton.

There was a gentle knock on my door. I looked at the clock. It was 11:00 P.M. Time for the private nurse I had ordered. I didn't really need one, but this was the first night. Someone just to be there, reading, writing letters, doing her nails, whatever—I didn't care.

The night nurse padded in. In the dim light, I could make out the white shoes, the blue cape, and the most glorious head of hair cascading down like an auburn Niagara. This angel of mercy came over to my bed.

"My name is Harvey. Anything I can do for you?"

I gasped! I couldn't help it. All that long, lovely, auburn hair going to waste. The cape? Oh, what the hell, this was San Francisco!

Somehow you don't associate San Francisco with hospitals. Maybe pasta, cable cars, Irish coffee, oral sex—but hospitals? No way. Too mundane. It sounds natural for someone to say "Fine hospital in Houston, Rochester, Topeka." All of these towns have a bedpan ring to them. But you just don't get sick in Baghdad-by-the-bay. The country's highest rate of alcoholism and suicide, yes. But sickness, no. If you get sick, go to Alameda or Oakland, but stay the hell out of San Francisco; that is, unless you're wearing a bell around your neck. But then, San Francisco always was a little hard to explain.

(CLICK)

The tapes. (I forgot to tell you, "Parky" and the tapes had come with me. No leaving them behind.)

Disassociated figures over which I had no control—rows of stark, similar houses ... a leering goat ... beckoning bathers on a rocky beach ... flowers weaving orgiastic patterns.

(TAPES)

(MEMORY BANK)

(CLICK)

(REWIND) "Hard to explain."

(CUE) 1953: Making the TV series "I Married Joan" with Joan Davis. In one episode, Joan's club is putting on a show. The leading lady gets sick. Joan's husband (that's me) pressed into service. Had to wear low-cut evening gown (an old one of Sophie Tucker's). Hair on chest peeking coyly over neckline. NBC's decision: too distasteful. Makeup man shaves hair from chest to follow neckline of dress. No more distastefulness for network. Left me with a heart-shaped hairy chest. After show, fast trip home to Ohio. Lunch with father at ultra-conservative Cleveland Athletic Club (last actor to sully its halls: Sir Harry Lauder). Father suggests a steam before two-martini lunch. We enter steam room. Stern-faced captains of industry, card-carrying Republicans all, sitting on hard wooden benches. Suddenly, as one, all eyes riveted on my heart-shaped chest. A cartel of stares at my Hester Pryne bosom. Father quickly sizes up situation.

"Let's get out of here, Son," he whispered. "You're hard enough to explain as it is."

(CLICK OFF)

Harvey, the nurse, came to my bedside. He handed me a sleeping pill with a water chaser. "If you need anything, I'll be over there doing my needlepoint."

Told you I would tell you how I happened to come to San Francisco, but I'm too tired. It's been a long day. I'll tell you tomorrow. My eyes are heavy. The tapes are mercifully stilled.

I took a last unbelieving look at Harvey-the-nurse, and I was able to make out the penciled motto for the sampler he was working on:

"DR. PARKINSON WAS A DRAG QUEEN."

3

L-Dopa

THE HOSPITAL CAME to life with the clatter of muffled dishes and muted bells. A young lady stuck her head in the door. Her blonde hair had been permed to stick straight out, and she sported a full theatrical makeup. I thought she was just visiting after doing an all-night show. That's what I thought, until she stuck a thermometer in my mouth and proceeded to take my pulse. She checked my vital signs, swung on a spike heel, and left. My mouth was still agape when Harvey returned from sneaking a look at my chart.

"Was that a nurse who was just in here?"

"Yes, it was," he said, and then he told me that in this androgynous infirmary, the personnel simply refused to wear uniforms; not even the nurses, not even their caps!

Harvey hummed a little tune as he gathered up his impedimenta. He was fresh as a daisy after a two-hour nap in the chair. He added that it was meditation, not medication. He emphasized that strange chemicals were poison to the body. What a tactful thing to tell me. Me, who was chock-full of L-Dopa; laced with Sinemet plus the residual of some chloral hydrate still churning around in my brisket.

I picked up Harvey's option for this night, too.

"I'll be back early tonight, and I'll bring some alfalfa sprouts and some barley bread."

Oh, God, what the hell am I doing here, I asked myself.

(CLICK)
(TAPES RETROGRESSIVE)
(PRESS)
(PLAY)

A few years ago I collapsed while making a TV series, "The Jim Backus Show." I was filming two half-hour shows every week. Pressures . . . unheard of hours . . . learning thirty to forty pages of dialogue every two days. Then, sudden panic: Flipsville! I took off like a Titan missile. Rick had scraped me off one of the floors of an MGM sound stage and incarcerated me at St. John's. A young psychiatrist named Tony had snapped me to my feet and had gotten me out of there and back to work in a miraculous three weeks. Truly a miracle! Oh, and let's not forget that when I didn't work, I was costing the network twenty-five thousand dollars a day.

Tony treated me for several years, and I was fine. From time to time, in strange situations, I would feel an attack of the "whips and jangles" coming on. I would phone Tony, who had moved to San Francisco, and after a few magic words, presto—I was okay! Don't ask me how he did it, but it worked.

Now he was one of the heads of this hospital. Rick, sensing that the word "Parkinson's" was about to loose a hurricane of anxiety in me, recommended that I check into Tony's hospital for a week. Tony would oversee the entire procedure and give me an hour of psychotherapy every day, while consigning three of his best Parkinson mavins on my body. And that's how I happened to be in a hospital in San Francisco.

(TAPES STILL ROLLING)

Evaluation!

Since I had been informed of my pox, I had picked up a load of information on Parkinson's, some from rather strange sources. It happens with every disease. Everyone I ran into knew someone who had it.

"My father-in-law's had it for ten years. 'Elvis, the Pelvis' we call him, ha-ha-ha—Shake, rattle, and roll!"

A blithe spirit I knew assured me of one *good* side effect of L-Dopa:

increased virility. Horny twenty-four hours a day! The only problem is you need a winch to hoist you on and off.

And another interested party added, "Have you tried urinating? Forget it!" He explained, "It's a disease affecting all of the muscles, and to pee you use a muscle. Same with talking. You have to exercise everything. Make faces in the mirror. Wiggle your tongue a lot."

(Oh, my God, not in San Francisco!)

They were all well-meaning experts. It's like everyone has two businesses: their own and show business.

The topper came with a TV commercial I saw for L-Dopa! It opened with an audio announcement. "This commercial is brought to you by Monsanto, the chemical company with a heart!"

(Long shot)

An obviously successful business lady is dismounting from a private plane and loping across the tarmac. She is carrying her briefcase.

(Medium shot)

Same lady entering an office building en route to an executive board room. She turns and faces camera.

(Close-up)

She smiles and says:

"I have Parkinson's disease."

She then explains that due to L-Dopa, the wonder drug, she is now operating at 95 percent efficiency.

How she kept her job while undergoing the initial jolts of L-Dopa, her teeth chattering like castanets, ricocheting off the wall of the home office, is carefully omitted. Don't forget, the lady in the commercial actually had to have Parkinson's. That's the law. She actually had to be taking L-Dopa. What bugged me about the lady in the commercial was that she was so smug and cheerful. She was oozing the impression that she owed it all to Monsanto. I hope her next commercial is for a feminine spray, and it shows her as the only female at a picnic given by the Hell's Angels.*

(Suppose someone gave a gang-bang and nobody came?)

---

*Hell's Angels: A paramilitary group of motorcyclists given to wearing Nazi helmets and foul leather jackets festooned with swastikas. Specialty: beating up defenseless old folks with bicycle chains. Their sexual mores would make Caligula blanch.

BACKUS STRIKES BACK

Truth in advertising.
"Did you know that Sara Lee has frozen buns?"
"Hell, I didn't even know her lips were chapped."
More truth in advertising.
"Try snorting Preparation H. It's a mind-shrinking experience."
And
"I've tried other brands of pacemakers, but every time I made love to my wife, the garage doors opened!"
(Close-up of announcer)
"And now, back to our feature film, *Chain Saw Vasectomy!*"
(CLICK)
(TAPE OFF)

4

I Hear Chimes

BEFORE MY ILLNESS had a tag on it, something a doctor could get his teeth into, I had what I guess must be considered early symptoms. Falling out of the car was one of them. I would try to get out of my car, and my muscles would lock halfway out so I would have to get out of the car headfirst. A strange symptom, but a guaranteed laugh-getter. Great at receptions or outdoor functions that were being televised live.

"Here comes Mr. Magoo! All you kiddies, look! Oh, look! Mr. Magoo just fell out of his car headfirst! Isn't Mr. Magoo a funny fellow!"

I always wanted to be a knockabout comic, but this was ridiculous!

But that was only one symptom.

THIS IS HENNY

One night, Jim and I were sharing a warm bubble bath and drinking champagne. It was a tradition. We were celebrating the anniversary of the day we met.

There we were, wallowing in all that warm frothy water. I was the first to clamber out. Jim took a last generous gulp of his champagne and proceeded to follow. Suddenly, with his left leg hanging out of the tub and his right leg in, he was frozen. He couldn't move. He commanded his brain to move his legs, but nothing happened. He panicked!

"Get me out of here," he yelled.

I rushed over to help. We tried together. I pulled and he pushed, but his legs were hopelessly locked. I dashed out to get some help, while Jimmy sank back deeper into the fast-receding bubbles.

THIS IS JIM

I was helpless, like a beached whale. I tried to relax with my duck, my sailboat, and my soapy fish.

Finally, she returned. Henny with her outside help! Staring at me sitting helplessly in that tub was a brawny fireman in full regalia.

I'm a perfectly normal man. I dig kinky sex like everyone else, and I've always had secret fantasies about a *ménage à trois*. But a fireman, wearing those boots and with that hose!

Just my luck, anyway. Comes the sexual revolution, and I'm out of bullets!

THIS IS HENNY

Praise the lord and pass the ammunition. Besides, sex after fifty is terrific, especially the one time in the winter!

THIS IS JIM

I was once again with the Whiz Kids for a final evaluation.

"These symptoms just won't do," said Dr. Korman. "They don't match our evaluation."

"What do you mean 'won't do'? Being rescued by the L.A. Fire Department from a bubble bath because my legs locked—isn't that a symptom?"

They shook their blow-dried heads gravely. I plunged on.

"And falling out of my car headfirst on national television? In front of Grauman's Chinese? That's like mooning the Vatican.* Think that's good for my image?"

"You see, Mr. Backus, yours is a classical case of Parkinson's; therefore, the symptoms must be classical, too."

Dr. Romaine joined the dialogue. "I'll tell you something. I could never read those symptoms at a seminar. I'd be laughed off the podium."

I could not believe what I was hearing.

---

*Mooning: A quaint custom popularized by Marlon Brando, which consists of daring to surreptitiously expose the bare behind under the most unlikely circumstances.

"Look, by classical symptoms, we mean tremors, shaking head, shuffling gait. Hell, you don't even shake! On second thought, we'll fill in the history ourselves."

Genuflecting toward Houston and Dr. Michael de Bakey, they left the room, calling, "We'll be in consultation, Nurse, and after that you can reach us at 'Ma Maison.'"

I could hear their extroverted chatter all the way down the hall.

"As I was telling Rogers and Cowan, I never should have bothered with Parkinson's. Clinically, yes. But P.R.-wise,* no."

"It's a tacky disease. Listen, they don't even have a telethon."

"Well, what are you going to do, Tom. All the other diseases are taken, even sickle cell anemia. Hey, what about herpes?"

"Too trendy."

I made my way to the nurses' cubicle for my parking validation.

She stuck her little head out.

"While I'm here, do you want me to fill out my Blue Cross forms?" I asked.

"Blue Cross? Oh, no, we're with American Express!"

I stumbled across the waiting room, almost tripping over that damn rug again as the Muzak segued into "Lazy Bones."

I needed this like Orson Welles needs a banana split.

A prominent attorney, known in the courts and brothels of our town as Silver Tongue Slatkin, came to see me in the hospital. He was a man known and feared in courtrooms throughout the land. A man equally at ease with the heads of state, B'Nai B'rith, or the OPEC nations. He brought me up to date on everything. He cheered me up. It was a marvelous visit.

As he was leaving, he said, "Don't worry, Jim, someday you're going to be all right."

An unfortunate choice of words.

Then he added, "My brother, Alvin, has what you have. Had it before they had that drug . . ."

"You mean L-Dopa? I just started on it."

"Sure helped my brother. He swears by it, once you get used to the dizziness, the nausea, and the banging noise in your head."

"I hear chimes."

---

*P.R.: Public relations—actually, a press agent with delusions of grandeur.

This conversation was great for me. I get side effects from soup.

Slatkin laughed nervously. "He talks better, too, now that he's on L-Dopa."

Go on, Silver Tongue, I thought, hang yourself.

"He can say," he continued, "'how are—how are—' clear as a bell. We're pulling for him. One of these days he'll get the 'you' out."

I just stared at him. The only time Silver Tongue shut his mouth was to change feet.

"We take him to all the restaurants—the Bistro, Chasen's, Matteo's. We don't mind. . . ."

"And he's welcome?"

"Oh, sure. As long as he brings his bib."

He plunged on, "He just got back from Hong Kong. Just like any normal man, like you and me. Well, maybe me . . ." he added weakly. "Had a suit made over there. A real bargain. Well, it cost him a little more."

"Why was that?"

"Well," he said expansively, "he had to pay the three guys that held him down while he was being fitted."

Now he was in full swing. "Bye, now. Still at the same address?" Then he topped himself. "Got something to send you. That is, if you ever get out of here."

He retreated out the door.

I had persuaded Harvey, the nurse with the hair, to come back to Los Angeles with us. We made a Montey Woolley wheelchair exit.

In a way, coming home was tough. I walked out to the bar overlooking the pool. The room reverberated with remembered laughter of long-gone parties. New Year's Eve. Edward G. Robinson insisting on the same chair. George Burns saying to the bartender, "Same martini as last year." David Wayne telling one of his dialect stories. Henry Fonda and Robert Mitchum quietly charming the room. And after every party, Henny and I having a nightcap, replaying the evening. The happy times. All of them gone because in a remote corner of my goddamned skull some cells had gone out of business. Sorry, don't call us. We'll call you.

I went to bed. I could hear Henny's and Harvey's laughter downstairs and the clinking of their drinks. You deserve a good time, darling. You've earned it, old girl. I closed my eyes. It had been a long day.

(CLICK)
(TAPE ON)
The tapes had made the trip, and they were home, too. A kaleidoscope
... a dog on a beach ... a field of corn ... a hotdog stand ... birds flying
aimlessly ... files of faceless men, marching.
(CLICK OFF)

I opened my eyes. On my bedside table, there was a drink. Harvey, no
doubt, had left it on the way to my john. The muted pleasure sounds
came sifting up from below. I had been warned not to mix booze and
L-Dopa. Screw those pompous medical asses! I picked up the drink and
gulped it.

All hell broke loose—*Stars and Stripes Forever* ... bagpipes ... *The
1812 Overture,* with cannons!

I can't stand the booze, but I love the music!

5

Aloha

(CLICK)
(TAPE ON SOFTLY)
When the tapes played, I could lie back and observe, view it impersonally. It wasn't happening to me but to someone who looked like, felt like, me. A surrogate "me," through whom all the pain and joy were filtered.

Slowly, 1956 sneaked in.

Henny and I. New Year's Eve in New Orleans—a private club in the Latin Quarter. Mayor Chip Morrison hosting the governor of Tennessee; Frank Clement and his wife, Ceil; Happy Chandler; Estes Kefauver of the raccoon cap and his wife, Nancy; and us. It was corn-pone time in Dixie. "Hee Haw" with champagne. "Auld Lang Syne," y'all, "Happy New Year, Henny darling!" The kiss—a very tender, special kiss, as I was leaving in the morning.

New Year's night. Sitting with my lovely sister, Kate, on the porch of her pre-American-Revolution house atop the highest hill in the Bahamas. The orange moon lazily dipping into the lagoon like a fluorescent wafer. The sound of the steel drums. (A badly tuned jazz band whipping up "Just One More Time," drifting our way from the Harbour Island Club.) Katy and I had looked in on the members earlier. Emigrés from Britain and Canada sitting around drinking. Celebrating another year of remittance checks. "Long live the Queen!" Men with regimental ribbons, walrus mustaches covering roquefort teeth. Pushing hearty milk-giving wives in batik evening gowns and comfortable shoes in time to the music.

Katy had said, "These fools carry on like this till Twelfth Night. Take me home, Jimmy. I'm tired."

Walking together up the luminous white path. A greeting from a bobby's smiling black face—red tunic, white helmet—sing-song Calypso dialect, "Happy New Year, Mrs. Spencer. Tell the Mister thanks for my Christmas check." He saluted her with his baton. She reached out and touched his gloved hand.

Katy and I had our own private drink and toast.

"Know you'll be catching the morning plane. Say good-bye to me now, Jimmy. I'll be sleeping late. The doctor from Miami gets in around noon."

Thank God I had come.

January 16 was a cold, briny day. After my visit with Katy, I had gone back to New Orleans to do a show. Now the Sunset Limited was some thirty-six hours out. After gliding through the orange groves of San Bernardino and Pomona, the streamliner, last of a vanishing breed, ground its way to an unwilling halt in Los Angeles.

It had been an uneventful train trip, one I usually looked forward to. The fine Creole cooking on board, the heavy napery, the gumbo, the shrimp remoulade, the Ramos fizzes. Where did it all go? We had it, and we blew it.

I remember sitting in the club car when the papers came on at El Paso. The headline: BOGART DIES.

That night, its lonesome whistle wailing, the Sunset Limited made its way through western Texas. I sat in the club car drinking till closing.

As the train nudged its way into Union Station, I was nursing a gigantic hangover and an equally large Bloody Mary. I saw Henny on the platform. That was unusual. I generally took a cab while she waited at home. Then a hot shower, pajamas, and Henny in a negligee waiting before the open fire—another of our traditions.

Later, as we sat before the fire, I realized I was fairly drunk. Then, oddly for my wife, she mixed me a large Scotch and soda without my asking for it. She hesitated a moment, and, after I took a few sips, she said, "Katy's gone . . . today."

The fire hissed.

Thank God I had made that trip in time.

Henny left me alone. I sat staring straight ahead. Katy, my precious sister. Gone, I drank with firm intent. Erase the bad memories; reverse those tapes! Katy, Mother, Dad . . . all in the past year. I raised my drink.

To the Sunset Limited. To Katy. To Bogie. To gumbo. To Ramos fizzes! My drink spilled on the hearth.

Three days later, the men came and got me.

I remember sitting in the admitting room of the Aloha Sanitarium, a faceless, one-story building that squatted like an adobe toad in the east end of the San Fernando Valley. What a name for an establishment that is dedicated to the permanent rehabilitation of alcoholics and allied pill-heads. The Aloha—"Till we meet again." How prophetic!

I vaguely recall saying good-bye to Henny and being handed over to a nurse who looked like the winner of an Ernest Borgnine look-alike contest. The Aloha had once been a "hot-bed motel," and the decor remained the same with the exception of hospital beds, and bars on the windows. (Not to keep people out, but to keep them in!) Once you left the protective custody of a loved one and the cash-in-advance was handed over, the door closed, and you were theirs—just another drunk to be treated with all the dignity of a steer in a Chicago *abbattoir*.

I was stripped, searched, and unceremoniously poured into a hospital gown. Now, so many years later, I can still feel the humiliation and the grim humor. Henny had packed my overnight bag as though I were checking into the Ritz. Among the items was a huge alligator-trimmed flask of Chanel No. 5. This was grabbed by the nurse and was about to join my disappearing clothes.

"You'll never learn, will you? You lushes are all alike."

"But it's only perfume," I protested, "why are you taking it?"

"Because you'll drink it, that's why!"

With that, she spied a bottle of Soil-Off standing on the washbasin and added that to her contraband. Ever have a Soil-Off on the rocks? How about a Windex martini? It gives you a hell of a hangover, but your eyes are clear.

"Okay, Buster, roll over!" she commanded.

I looked at her blankly. Sensing that I was a new boy, she shoved me down on the bed and plunged a needle into my butt. She had the touch of a blacksmith. The last thing I remember was that Harpy of Mercy taking a last check from the doorway, silhouetted against the harsh light from the hall, as 75 cc's of paraldehyde raced to my brain.

Some thirty-six hours later, I surfaced.

I surfaced through a sea of morphine and paraldehyde. Their procedure, time tested—keep the patient zonked out. I flew through the sound barrier . . . Mach I . . . the Whips . . . the Whammies . . . the Frantication. The only recollection of that thirty-six hours was emerging from that devil's sleep, flailing and straining against the straps. Finally, blessed darkness—peopled with demons on the edge of my dreams. All of this was added and filed with my tapes.

Much later, I was prodded out of my bed. I donned my robe and slippers and joined my fellow zombies in the common room, a rather bare room with chairs and tables covered with overflowing ashtrays, papers, and dog-eared copies of *Argosy, Motor Age,* and *Field & Stream.* The television set, which seemed wired to "Billy Graham" and "All Star Bowling," was blaring away and the room was in constant motion. The pajama-clad patients, pacing, sitting only briefly. Conversation sparse, just endless shuffling. Most of them were repeaters who patiently accepted this pit stop on the road to oblivion. The turnover was endless, new accolytes joining the *Ballet Mechanique,* falling into the rhythm instinctively. It was as if we belonged to an order of flagellants bound for self-immolation.

There was a mystic bond between the inmates and their keepers. Why not? The jailers were AA, which made them only one drink removed from the prisoners. Like the strange affinity between cop and criminal, prostitute and pimp.

During the week I spent there, I have no recollection of ever sitting down to eat. I know I was fed somehow. Fed their great dollops of gravy-drenched entrées and monolithic slabs of rice pudding.

From what I gleaned out of the scraps of conversation, most of the inmates were successful males, a mélange of businessmen, society men, remittance men and one airline captain. All seemed to have reached a détente with their loved ones, as visitors were few and far between.

The next afternoon, I was suddenly awakened from a Rip Van Winkle nap. I had heard someone enter. (Privacy was an unknown commodity.) I opened my eyes and saw one of the screen's most honored and respected actors. He was tanned, healthy—a tower of sobriety. Mom's apple pie, "Jingle All the Way," "Out to Old Aunt Mary's." I almost unraveled. Oh, my God, I thought. I'm being censured by the Screen Actors Guild. I'm being excommunicated from the performing arts!

"Hi," he said cheerfully. "I see you've got my old room."

I stared at this handsome, wholesome, smiling man who looked as if he were designed by Walt Disney. He sat down on the chair beside my bed. He talked. I listened. And I didn't have another drink for more than eight years.

(CLICK)

(TAPE OFF)

6

Cope-ulation

THIS IS HENNY

RICK HAD EXPLAINED it to us. Chapter and verse. The way back would be tough, discouraging, and, at times, seemingly hopeless. No two cases are alike. No two reactions to the medication even similar. He outlined the program.

I took Jim to a physiotherapist three times a week, a cheerful young man who kneaded and massaged his muscles and tendons in a never-ending race against Dr. Parkinson and his forces of evil. Then came a workout with strange contraptions, lying full length, manacled into place, pulling on a stirrup connected to different size weights—all tugging against him with various tensions. The huge room was filled with chairs, tables, and slant boards oozing wires, chains, and straps. It looked like the rumpus room of the Marquis de Sade. Jim wondered why the hell he hadn't done this twenty years ago when it could have done his body some good. Now it was just a holding action.

This therapy took care of Monday, Wednesday, and Friday.

In his leisure time, Tuesday, Thursday, Saturday, and Sunday—a four- to five-mile walk. Then forty-five minutes in our heated pool. Although Jim had been a champion swimmer, he had lost the ability to coordinate his arms and legs. Sometimes one of his legs would lock, sometimes both. So he could no longer swim the *length* of the pool. Instead, he would swim the width in the shallow end. At first he could only go four widths and would come up gasping. "Kick those legs. Kick those legs," I'd shout. (A Parky uses four times normal energy in order to do the simplest things.) "Kick those legs! O.K.?"

"Get out of the pool, lover. Your lips are blue." (A bad joke, but anything to cheer him up.)

Then came his hour of singing to exercise the throat and lips.

In between, I instructed him in exercises from the *Parkinson Rehabilitation Manual,* which I hid from my hypochondriac husband. Page after page of them. For every little part of the body: the neck, the fingers, the toes, the heels, each accompanied by a helpful hint.

"Tower to patient.

"'When turning, never pivot in a spot. Your feet should be kept apart and the turn should be made in a large arc and always in a forward direction. During turning you should avoid crossing your feet. Plan your turn in order to have adequate room to complete the arc.'

"Over and out.

By the book. Loud and clear!

"Talking while you walk may interfere with your balance. If you need to say something while you are walking, stop, say what you need to say, then resume walking."

(Explain *that* to a director!)

Poor darling Jimmy, his instinct was to withdraw from the world. Only one problem: prior to the evaluation, when he had difficulty walking and felt self-conscious with people, he would fortify himself with a few drinks. That way he could make it through the evening.

Now he was tagged a "Parky." He had a label. He was under medication. Liquor was out. His crutch was a no-no. He was *safe* here at home, away from the world.

Thank God he was between commitments. He turned down the talk shows. There was no way he could have done them.

He was in constant pain, utter terror. It made him so weak that even driving a car became a problem. *Everything* was a problem. All the simple little things we do each day without giving them a thought turned into major obstacles. George Burns once told me, "The secret of staying young is 'Don't fall in love with your bed.'" Jim wallowed in his. Any excuse to stay there, curled in the fetal position. Here he was truly safe.

Jim, who is one of our great raconteurs, had always been in demand for dinners, benefits, charities, and to emcee and introduce dignitaries. Suddenly he was a no-show. The papers, the media became curious. What was the matter? Was he sick? One of the more notorious scandal sheets called the house. I happened to answer the phone, thank God.

A cheery voice at the other end said, "This is *The National Enquirer.*"

"Yes," I said, "what can I do for you?"

He said, "Hey, Mrs. Backus, we hear Jim's dying. Care to comment?"

I hung up on him. I was terrified. Maybe they knew something.

One day, a dear friend of ours called just to say hello. I pledged her to secrecy and told her Jim had Parkinson's disease.

"How utterly divine!" she exclaimed. "I had three lovers with that. Tell me, does he have those simply marvelous tremors? Once I was making love with a famous composer. Well, my dear, he started to quiver and shake. I was so flattered. I thought it was me. Turned out to be you-know-what!" She giggled at the memory.

THIS IS JIM

I got hold of the Parkinson pamphlet behind Henny's back. Its purpose is to instruct and encourage the "patient," or "victim." Now, there is a choice of words. To me, a "patient" is someone propped up on a chaise lounge looking very pale and wan, writing sad poems with a feather. A "victim," however, is someone who is trapped at a Chill Wills film festival without a cyanide ticket.

The pamphlet also encourages you to continue participating in golfing, tennising, bowling, jousting, wenching, boating, or whatever tickled your fancy before you got the pox. "Get with it!" it urges. Oh, sure! A Parky in a foursome playing a ten dollar Nassau with automatic presses is as welcome as a hernia at a weight lifters' convention. (Come to think of it, the last time I played golf I hit *two* balls. I stepped on a rake.)

As for boating—now there's an archaic phrase. When is the last time you heard someone say, "I spent the weekend boating." I sailed two broads over to Catalina, maybe, but boating?

And! As for hunting, this most rugged of sports, it's charm has always escaped me. Going gunning for doves. Gunning for doves? Those dear little feathered creatures, those symbols of tender love? Why the very word "dove" conjures up memories. First love . . . the Junior Prom . . . wrist corsages . . . romantic dalliances! How about the *hazards* of hunting? You might get shot by a deer and wind up draped over the hood of a '58 Chevy. I once, and only once, went on a hunting trip, and I well remember another hazard. We had a cabin in the High Sierras. Everything was very macho. Lots of barrack's humor, peeing your name in the snow, sleeping two in an upper bunk like GIs on a troop train, your feet in his face and vice versa. You have to be very careful of that. You can wind up with a terrible case of athlete's nose!

7

Alcoholic Chic

"NO BOOZE!"

That was the unanimous decision. Rick, Tony, the three Parkinson mavins in San Francisco; even Frick and Frack, the Whiz Kids, agreed. In their case "agreed" was too common a word. "Concurred." That was more Cedars-Sinai.

(TAPES)
(CLICK ON)

Cedars-Sinai. The celebrity floor. The eighth floor. 1974. George Burns in an oxygen tent after his heart-bypass surgery. I was allowed to visit. It was the first time I had ever seen him without a cigar. What to say? Finally, "How was it, George?"

He opened one eye and looked at me owlishly. "Not as bad as playing Akron."

And Edmund Gwenn (who will always be Santa Claus) was well into his nineties as he lay on the eighth floor, wafting in and out of a coma. He had shuffled off this mortal coil several times, only to drift back to life. When he was asked what it was like to cross over, he replied, "Not as bad as playing comedy."

Actors! We're all alike.
(TAPES)
(CLICK OFF)

A life of total abstinence? That was like trying to envision eternity!
Too much to comprehend. "One day at a time," they counseled. "Easy
does it!" It was no help. I lay there in a panic.

(CLICK)
(TAPES ON)
(RETROGRESSIVE)
January 1956. My first Alcoholics Anonymous meeting. Fresh out of
the Aloha, I was taken by the hand by that wholesome, G-rated actor
whose room I had had at the Aloha. These were very secret meetings held
in the playhouse on his Beverly Hills estate. I couldn't believe he was ever
a drunk. Last person ever! You'd think of him as having, at the most, two
fingers of applejack out of a tin cup as he bedded down his steed, kicked
a little shit, and kissed the schoolmarm goodnight.

I was very nervous.

About twenty-five men were sitting around a huge table, chain smoking and drinking innumerable cups of coffee. I recognized at least ten
pals from my forays up and down the Sunset Strip who had disappeared
out of my life. So this was where they were! I was terribly shaky.

"Hi, Jim."

No big deal. No "What are *you* doing here?" None of that.

The rest of the group were guys I had worked with or whose faces I
recognized. Most of them were actors. At this time, Hollywood was still
a company town. To the studio heads, drunks were anathema. Alcoholics were visible! Not only were they visible, what was more important,
they *held up production*! Even Louella's own alcoholic, her husband,
Docky, had recently been very visible. He'd gotten soused in Chasen's,
and, as he slid under the table, she simpered, "Don't wake him up! He's
got to operate in the morning!"

(TAPES STILL ROLLING)
A few years before, five big stars had formed this AA splinter meeting
out of necessity. For them, anonymity was a must. Through the years,
the meeting had grown. Seated around the table now were the original
five, plus a lovable old-timer who conjured up memories of sarsaparilla,

girls with pigtails, and dogs with rings around their eyes who smoked pipes. The homespun roles for which this revered old actor is remembered were a far cry from the lurid tales he told at meetings about Skid Row and padded cells.

Three noted writers were sitting together, one of whom was synonymous with Biblical spectacles. To round out the membership, we also had two priests who were bucking for bishop, and one lone rabbi— sacramental winos.

Insidiously, week by week, the number of attendees grew. It took a while to figure it out. Hollywood drunks, wet or dry, have relatives from out of town who want to see movie stars. So the relatives would comb the beach at Santa Monica. They would stroll down Hollywood Boulevard. They would go to the Brown Derby. No movie stars.

One day, a makeup man on a picture happened to overhear one of our boys talking about our secret meetings. What a great idea! So he came up to the meeting, bringing with him his star-starved visiting uncle. The word was out. It didn't take long. Soon the playhouse was jammed with workers in the industry with their visiting kin ogling the drunks and getting autographs on plastic coffee cups.

One night, at the height of this period, the door opened, and there stood Jack Lemmon. I leapt up to greet him. We had snared a biggie!

"Jack, good to see you!"

"Hi, Jim."

"Gee, Jack, I didn't know you were a drunk!" I whispered.

"Are you out of your mind?" he muttered through clenched teeth. "I'm here to do research for *Wine and Roses!*"

It was a night to remember. Later that same evening, the doors were flung open, and in burst a gorgeous woman. Every eye was on this international, controversial, unpredictable star of dubious reputation as she crashed her way into the meeting and took stage on our little platform. She raised her hands high and said in her unforgettable baritone, "Gentlemen, I am wounded to the core! Never have any of you asked me to one of your meetings, and I have been a guest at the Garrick, the Players, the Lambs', and, besides, this is my birthday. One year ago tonight, I had my last drink! You know, for years I had heard about Alcoholics Anonymous, and for years I knew that I should join your little club, but I was afraid you were all such do-gooders and all so terribly moral. It wasn't till I did join AA that I realized you really wouldn't care a damn if I fucked a snake, as long as it was sober!"

Well, that's what makes AA work. The speeches the members make.
They are sometimes hilarious, sometimes heartrending, certainly always
fascinating. Drunks are gregarious and generally articulate. The "civil-
ians" were better than the "pros," for the most part, and the simple way
they told of their experiences would sometimes tear your guts out.

It wasn't the relatives who did us in, or the lady who crashed, or even
the fact that there was no longer enough room in our meeting hall. It was
the tour buses. That idiotic Hollywood institution of buses filled with
avid sightseers cruising up and down the streets of Beverly Hills and
Bel-Air like so many hungry sharks.

We were not exactly choked up when we emerged from a Sunday
afternoon meeting just in time to see our first tour bus slow down and
hear the voice of a leather-lunged guide blare from the loudspeaker, "On
the right is the movie stars' branch of Alcoholics Anonymous. Uh-huh!
Here they come now. If you look carefully, keep your eyes open, maybe
you can see one of your favorites."

Naturally, we couldn't disappoint our fans, so we all pretended to
throw up in the bushes.

Well, we deserved it. In our quest for anonymity, we had violated the
first precept of AA. "The door must always be open to anyone who needs
help." Once you forget that, you're one drink away from disaster.

What happened to the playhouse group? Four have disappeared, five
have died, two are hopelessly insane, and I am writing this with a pen
stuck in a potato.

Drink up, everybody!
(CLICK)
(TAPES OFF)

8

A Parrot on His Shoulder

WHEN RICK TOLD me I needed to go back into psychotherapy, I thought (reluctantly) he had a point. I had retreated from the world. Gone into a closet and pulled Henny in with me on a self-imposed exile. (Poor darling Henny—the scourge of Magnin's, the jovial hostess. She hadn't been out of the house in months. She waited on me hand and foot, and though I was not incontinent, I was certainly the next thing to it.)

Okay, I agreed to go, but to whom? Tony was up in San Francisco. I had tried that route. Traveling nine hundred miles round trip for fifty minutes of treatment three times a week was too much for the id, not to mention the ego.

As for the Bedford Drive cabal, no thanks! I'd had that. Why are 99 percent of all the analysts in Los Angeles crammed together in that couch-lined casbah in Beverly Hills? Why must they all be on Id Row? With their maze of offices, it's like an insane rabbits' warren, all exactly alike—little cubicles adjoining tiny treatment rooms. The whole place is a teeming bazaar of well-heeled neurotics. Even Pepe LeMoko would get lost in there!

As for parking on that street, they don't park the car, they hold it for ransom. The parking boy couldn't care less. To him, it's only a temporary job till some Arab sheik gets a load of his tight little denim ass and takes him out of all that.

At ten minutes to the hour, on cue, all the little analysts, like so many Dorso-clad moles, step out of their holes for a breath of air. Then back to their modules to fuck up somebody else to a fare-thee-well. They got Marilyn. I wonder who's next?

Rick assured me this analyst was different. He and Tony had been residents together at the best-known psychiatric clinic in the country. He had moved his office, Rick said, to his house in the hills overlooking the Pacific, with peace and quiet, no parking hassles, and no claustrophobic cubicle. Okay, I'd give it a try.

I drove out Sunset to Pacific Palisades, made a left, and drove down a quiet, tree-lined, residential street. There it was. No problem. I parked right at the curb. I looked at the house. It was a large Mediterranean ranch house of faded elegance, in the old Hollywood style. I peered around at the garage and half expected to see Erich von Stroheim hosing down a vintage Rolls Royce Landau. I could see a huge courtyard in the back, shaded by a tremendous, ancient magnolia tree, whose branches and giant white blooms spread like a parasol over most of the area. What a great place for fiestas! I could visualize the senoritas, the piñatas, and the peon at the pit, barbecuing an ox.

Around the corner of the house came a tousled giant of a man with a craggy face and an unruly mop of reddish-gray hair. He was dressed like a retired rancher. He spied my car and made his way over, walking with a rolling gait like a sea captain. No, more like a retired pirate. All he needed was a parrot sitting on his shoulder.

His office was the old chauffeur's suite in the back of the garage, with a view of Santa Monica Bay. Now this made sense!

Last week I had told Rick, okay, I would go see another analyst, but I was doing it under duress. The protest flag was up—a handkerchief on the play. Then I explained to him once again, "Look, Rick, I've been this route before. First in New York, with Fania. She was a strict Freudian, remember? Never talked to you. Only spoke two words: "Hello" and, six years later, "Good-bye.""

"But she got the job done."

"Yes," I reluctantly agreed, "I guess so."

"And you're forgetting Tony?"

"No, Rick, far from it. He saved my life."

It was true. Tony had my number. I remember once I had an anxiety attack in Munich. Ten minutes on the phone with Tony—magic! Even with a bad connection, which was filtered through a crossed wire full of *bittes* and *dankes*.

"But this is different, Rick, I've got Parkinson's. . . ."

Rick interrupted. "All the more reason. So much of any illness is psychosomatic."

I leapt to my feet. I was damned if I was going to give in easily.

"True," I told him, "just so this new guy knows he's dealing with a pro! And warn him I'm hip to that penis envy-sibling rivalry jive!"

"Sit down, Jimmy," Rick said kindly. "Don't worry, I'll warn him. I know he can handle it."

So here I was with a new doctor. He and I stalked each other like two fighters. Actually, he just lay back, and I did all the fancy footwork. Damned if I was going to be intimidated by a shrink.

Get the priorities in order, I thought, the ground rules worked out. What the hell, I'm paying him!

I circled his somewhat rustic office, suspiciously eyeing the decor. It was one thing to depart from the primitive African masks and the Picasso prints of Bedford Drive, but what was this? Frederic Remington? Yes, and with a tinge of Norman Rockwell and overtones of Teddy Roosevelt. Near the window were two comfortable-looking leather chairs opposite each other, with a fat hassock in between. Obviously we were to sit facing each other . . . just like Tony's office.

"No couch?" I growled.

"Lost in the fire."

"Chicago fire?" I asked sarcastically.

"No, Bel-Air."

He'd topped me. Score one for the analyst. He indicated the far chair.

"Mind if I smoke?" he asked.

I shrugged and sat down. He pulled out a thin cheroot. Oh, no, I thought to myself, what's with this Mark-Twain stogie? First, the Whiz Kids, and now, this day-player from the Warner Brothers' ranch.

I was staring at my new therapist when suddenly (as they always did) . . .

(CLICK)
(TAPES ON)

1965: I was playing the part of a psychoanalyst in a dream sequence in an MGM musical. I had argued and argued with its producer, Joe

Pasternack, who demanded that I wear a Van Dyke beard, a morning suit, and a pince-nez, while my crystal consulting room slowly revolved around a column of gorgeous, feathered Amazons. Maybe Joe Pasternack was right. After all, he *was* Hungarian!

(CLICK)

(TAPES OFF)

I blinked my eyes. The doctor, sensing my discomfort, lumbered to the window and half-closed the venetian blinds. I was glad. The view of the bay and dancing sailboats was too distracting, not in keeping with my murky psyche. Freud was smart. His office had overlooked a strudel factory.

We chatted about this and that for quite a while, just wasting time. I had to start somewhere. I plunged in.

"Well, ever since I've had Parkinson's, I've . . ."

He leaned forward. "What?"

I repeated, "Ever since I got sick and got Parkinson's disease. . . ."

He looked at me and took a drag on his cheroot. The smoke curled upward. He continued to stare like Walter Huston looking at Humphrey Bogart's Earl C. Dobbs character in *The Treasure of the Sierra Madre*.

"I've got Parkinson's," I patiently repeated.

"You mean you got something someone put a tag on."

"I don't get it."

He put down his stogie and explained, "They gave it a label, something for you to hang onto. They tagged it."

I half-knew what he was trying to tell me.

"You just bridled," he continued. "You seem determined to defend that tag."

I ignored his comments and plunged on.

"Okay, but ever since I've been tagged, I've gotten these damn fears. Groundless stupid fears. I anticipate all sorts of horrors. Two days in advance of just doing something simple, like meeting someone for lunch, I can see myself falling down and drooling or maybe not being able to talk—all my friends staring at me."

He pushed his ashtray away and leaned in closer.

"Well, you must never disappoint your friends. They expect it of you. If you've got that disease, Parkinson's, like you say you have, you've got to shake, rattle, and roll, or they'll never visit you and bring you their jams and jellies."

What's going on here, I thought. Is this shrink putting me on?

"No, you see. . . ." I was determined to get through to him. It was very important. "I play the whole lunch scene in my head way before the actual date. Like spilling the soup, or knocking over the table, or tripping over Irving Lazar.* The whole thing is so goddamned real and terrifying!"

He smiled at me. "That's because you're playing negative tapes."

He rose. The fifty minutes were up.

"See you Wednesday."

"Right."

It seemed so short. I was shaken by the abrupt termination of our session. I had wasted so much of the hour.

"See you Wednesday, Doctor—er—Doctor. . . ." I couldn't remember his name.

"Call me R.G."

He stomped to the door and courteously saw me out.

I stepped out into the dazzling sunlight and made my way to my car. I remembered the sense of relief I felt after one of those one-sided bouts with Fania back in New York—fifty minutes of agonizing gut-wrenching from me and dead silence from the other side of the couch. At least then I emerged into the teeming action of West Eighty-third Street with four bars, one on each corner. Take your ethnic pick. One belt to get earthside and another to get me through the emotional bends. Now, here I was standing in the middle of a Spanish land grant, where the deer and the antelope play, with my cranium stuffed full of that poor man's Antibuse, L-Dopa.

I turned the ignition key savagely.

I was playing negative tapes, was I? Fifty minutes to hear bullshit like that. Negative tapes? Tapes?

It hit me with the wollop of a pile driver. That craggy, gimpy son-of-a-bitch! How did he know about my tapes. Nobody knew. Not even Henny. I never told Rick. Not even Tony. Nobody knew but me. And now he did, R.G.!

WHAT *WERE* THOSE MYSTERIOUS TAPES?

I roared off in search of the nearest cantina.

---

*Irving Lazar: A famous literary agent—stands all of 5'3" in his argyle feet.

9

From Natchez to Mobile

THIS IS HENNY

JIMMY HAS ALWAYS been the world's greatest hypochondriac. In his salad days, when he was happy to grace podiums for any worthwhile cause, he took on the symptoms of whatever disease they were plugging. It made me wonder if he really *did* have Parkinson's disease.

For example, one morning right after his appointment with R.G., he turned on his car radio to listen to his favorite program, "Medical News in Review." He knew better, but he couldn't help it. He was insidiously trapped, the same way that, knowing better, you keep probing your sore tooth with your tongue.

THIS IS JIM

Yes, I should have known better. That day the host of the show announced that there was a new virulent strain of an old social disease imported from Vietnam that had hit our shores and was now achieving epidemic proportions among teenagers. Alas—just as we were about to relegate Cupid's catarrh to limbo along with TB and the hula hoope.

(TAPES)
(SWITCH ON)

(BLACK AND WHITE)

Circa 1938. I was an apprentice radio announcer in Cleveland, Ohio, with a take-home pay of $22.50 a week. One of my more pleasurable chores was doing a remote. (A "remote" is a broadcast from any place other than the actual radio station.) My remotes were generally directly from the bandstand of a dance hall, a restaurant, or a night club, usually late at night. I went from one upholstered sewer to another, in sheer ecstacy!

I stood on that bandstand and, with my ear carefully cupped in true announcer style, intoned, "Hi there! From the Lotus Garden Restaurant high atop Playhouse Square in downtown Cleveland, we bring you the music of Emerson Gill and his orchestra. And now, stepping mikeside is Pinky Hunter to ask the musical question "Who?""

Now, mind you, if I said "From *Charley Ten's* Lotus Garden Restaurant," that was good for a free chow mein dinner, hopefully for two. The Lotus Garden was a habitat for filing clerks who worked late. Girls dancing with girls was de rigueur. Boys, however, dancing with boys was greeted with a fast trip to the Bastille.

In my announcement, if I said "the *incomparable* music of Emerson Gill and his men of music," the maestro would surreptitiously reward me with a pint of gin and a bottle of Tom Collins mix.

How sweet it was!!

One summer's night, a full moon found me on the bandstand, my ear carefully cupped. "Hi there. This is James Gilmore Backus coming to you from high atop Willowick Country Club on the shores of beautiful Lake Erie, bringing you the irresistible music of Sammy Kaye. And now, here's our maestro stepping mikeside to tell you about his first toe-tapping medley."

I cut quite a romantic figure, drenched in that magenta spotlight— bisquit-brown sports jacket, striped flannel trousers, and white buckskin shoes—which caused every female heart to trip. There was something about my charismatic stint that acted as a hell of an aphrodisiac. Prior to this job, the only dates I could get were with Catholic girls during Lent.

After "This is James Gilmore Backus bidding you good night," I found myself at a table with some of Cleveland's more eligible bucks and their pedigreed doxies. I was sitting next to a lovely visitor from the South, one Cindy Lou Emma Bessie Clay Calhoun. In tones redolent of chitlins and corn pone, she informed me that she was visiting her college roommate for a few days, then would be returning to Natchez by way of

Mr. Magoo and his two Oscars, as seen on "Person to Person"
(Courtesy CBS, UPA Pictures)

On location for *Magic Carpet*, Florence, Italy

Playing the Coliseum, same movie

Playing ourselves in M.G.M.'s *Don't Make Waves*—Tony who? (M.G.M. Studios)

Did Jim say something naughty? "This Is Your Life." (Courtesy Ralph Edwards Productions)

Jim substituted for a number of years for Dave Garroway, the original "Today" show host, during the month of August. Left to right: Jack Lescoulie, Charles Van Doren, Betty Ann Grove, Henny, Jim (Courtesy Raimondo Borea)

"Take it off, Jim. You're hard enough to explain without it."
(Courtesy Doré Records)

Hosting the Children's Hospital telethon: Henny with her
favorite instrument—the telephone. (Bing Crosby Productions)

Jim's act, Las Vegas, 1979
(Courtesy Fremont Hotel)

Jim and his furry friend, Las Vegas. "Inside that gorilla suit is another gorilla." (Courtesy Freemont Hotel)

"Couldn't help, couldn't hurt." Jim and his dance instructor, Tybee. (Photo by Robert Landau)

Our house, New Year's Eve, 1979. Richard and one of the Mrs. Burtons. (Photo courtesy Nate Cutler)

(opposite page) The "Mike Douglas Show" two years ago, while quite ill (Michael Leshnov Photography)

Thanksgiving, 1981: George Burns, Jack Carter, Jim, and Henny

February 1983: Henny with the author of the Foreword

Auld Lang Syne, 1983, with old chums Gloria and Donald O'Connor, chez Backus (Nate Cutler Photo)

David Wayne with the author of the Foreword and Jim and
Henny (Photo courtesy Nate Cutler)

Mobile, "wherever the four winds blow," to wed Captain Beuregarde Clayton Jackson and Durante.

Some three Green-River-and-bourbons later, I was somehow strolling along the shores of Lake Erie, hand in hand with this pantalooned vixen. Sinking into the sand, she gathered in her voluminous organdy skirt and made room for me to sit close to her. The moon, the lake—they worked their insidious magic. Cindy Lou was mine for the taking, but how? To disrobe this flower of the South was no easy matter. She was bundled into a formidable array of garments: petticoats, a chemise, a waist cinch, a bra—all of them hung with those little sachet bags. Thanks to the medical fact that a man reaches his sexual peak at nineteen, I was able to perform that task without losing my ardor. At last!

Distant thunder.

The whistle of a steamer!

Sky rockets exploding!

And in the distance, a band blaring "Bonaparte's Retreat!"

Nine days later I was announcing "Betty Lou Taylor and her mighty Wurlitzer." The vibrations from Betty Lou's mighty organ seemed to be doing strange things to the lower part of my body, so I quickly made my way to the men's room. It was in the men's room of Station WTAM (50,000 watts) that I was confronted with stark reality. I was damaged goods! A lifetime of regret for one moment of ecstacy. Cindy Lou had struck back! General Sherman's revenge! The South shall rise again!

Dr. Pomeroy took me into his office.

"Now, Jim, the main thing is your mental approach to this thing. Remember, you are not alone. As a doctor, I can't mention names, but, everyone . . . even the mayor . . . I mean, talk this over with your dad. Knowing Russ, he'll understand. Remember what I told you. There is no stigma."

He rose, put on a rubber glove, and shook my hand.

Pop understood. But he had just a few ground rules: eat off separate plates, sleep in the garage, don't kiss your mother, "and stay the hell away from my clients!"

(TAPES CLICK OFF)

The radio was blaring. A disk jockey was chattering away. I switched to an FM station. Ah, that was better, a Cole Porter medley. The announcer interrupted quietly, tastefully. That was more like it. This was my kind of music. I drove on listening to "Night and Day." I was interrupted by thoughts of that tape that had just finished playing in my head. How much of it was true? How much was fantasy? Even the tapes could lie. What had just unreeled was the way I had always wished it had been. I guess I had twisted it until it became my illusion—telling it, retelling it, playing it, replaying it, cutting it, trimming everything away from the distasteful truth, unable to face the way it really was. What a life, based on a stream of one-liners.

In my session with R.G., I had developed a technique of clicking on, verbalizing, stopping, reviewing, clicking forward, checking. Where did the tapes end and reality begin? R.G. had explained the word "tapes" to me. They were nothing new, nothing peculiar only to me, and now, by some quirk of fortune, understood by him. For other people, there were different tags. "Cassettes," maybe. In other times, "daydreams," "fantasies," "Walter Mittyisms."

As it was now, the tapes controlled me and my emotions. They had the power to elate me—positive tapes. They could plunge me into the pits—negative tapes. Since my illness (we never used its name), the tapes were my masters.

For example, a negative tape might go like this: Let us say today was Monday and I was scheduled to start shooting a picture on Wednesday. I would immediately start projecting ahead. I would be late, I wouldn't know my lines, in the middle of a speech my mouth would go dry, or worse, my tongue would drown in my saliva—I would drool! This part wasn't a fantasy. It was a true Parkinsonism.

"There I said it! Goddamn it, R.G. It's right in the Parkinson manual! That and the . . . and the . . . and the. . . ."

"Jim, turn off that negative tape!"

"What do you mean, R.G.? Play positive tapes? Make them up?"

"Why not? They're both figments. . . ."

"Sure. Guess you're right. Fabricate, don't franticate, right? Okay, it's Tuesday. A beautiful day. Things are going flawlessly. No, it's not true! Well, neither are the others, the negatives. The whole thing is a lie! And the picture starts shooting only twenty-four hours away! Bring it down to the moment. Live for the moment. Now! But how? Please, dear God, tell me how? R.G., show me!"

I had pulled off the road. I was shaking, sobbing softly. I sat there. What to do?

Play an old tape. That's what I'll do. They were safe. They had been filed and documented. I'll play a funny tape. So what if it was mostly fabrication. It'll make me laugh.

I turned into the Bel-Air gate and drove down the street to my driveway, parked my car, and opened the front door. From upstairs came her voice.

"Darling, is that you?"

All the tapes stopped. I stopped too. This was *it*. This was *now*. This was of the moment. Enjoy it, Jim! The gleam of light at the end of a long tunnel.

"Henny, take my hand. Show me the way."

10

In the Rough

I SAT STARING at R.G. and wishing I could get out of his office. The fifty minutes were almost up, so why didn't I leave now and go over to the club? I was about to do just that when, without any warning, I started thinking about golf and what the Riviera Country Club was like when I first joined.

These days, the Riviera is the polyester playground of incorporated dentists and Santa Monica burghers. It's a far, far cry from the verdant fairways of 1947, when its timbered clubhouse boasted the greatest mélange of golf hustlers, tosspots, and fancy men this side of Port Said. On any given day, you might see Three-Iron Gates, who would play anyone for any sum, using only his redoubtable three-iron, the Count, complete with spiked dancing pumps and monocle, who was known to leave the premises after a day of golf and gin rummy some thousands of dollars richer and Victor Mature, known as the "Beautiful Hunk of Man." His masculine endowments were right up there with the Sistine Chapel and the Colossus of Rhodes. He would play his daily seventy-two holes of golf, followed by his faithful dog, Genius. One day, at the end of nine holes, he ordered Genius up the hill to the clubhouse. When I asked him why, he said, "Genius has developed a wheeze, and his doctor says his heart is bad. He can play only nine holes a day." Genius went to his Maker secure in the knowledge that Dr. Christian Barnard had done his best.

It is *indeed* a far cry from those halcyon days when you were apt to see a foursome consisting of the lower-case Marx brother; a gaunt, sneaker-shod Howard Hughes; an identifiable Don of the Costa Nostra; and Mickey Rooney, fresh out of knickers and his latest bride.

I came out of my reverie and continued to stare at R.G. I was startled by the clarity of my memories. They brought into focus how much golf had meant to me, how much a part of me it had been.

Sure, some of it was macho bullshit, but did R.G. know that? Was I getting through to him? What impact did my tapes have on him, any-way? Did he write them all down in his log after I left? (That's right, "log." It had come up in a crossword puzzle.)

How could I impress on him that I wasn't just some golfing idiot from the club across the way with a galloping case of Parkinson's disease?

"I used to be a hell of a golfer, R.G."

He nodded. I sat back and thought about it some more.

"Listen, R.G., when I was a kid I wanted to be a golf pro. My father wanted it for me, too, as long as I got an education. I grew up on a golf course. Our house was right on the third fairway. My father was a pretty good golfer. When other kids were tossing a ball at each other or scuffing a stone with their shoe, I was shagging golf balls. Old Kroflites, using a cut-down mashie that once belonged to Bobby Jones.

"When I was fourteen, my father said, 'You've got a good shot to win the Lakeland title.' I still have the cup, R.G. It's on the mantel in the den. 'Jimmie' (they spelled my name wrong) 'Backus, Junior Champion.' It was shown on TV, that cup, along with some of my other golf trophies and my two Oscars—on 'Person to Person.'"

He didn't say a word, just looked at me. I wondered if I was getting through to him at all.

"Edward R. Murrow came to our house to do 'Person to Person' the week after Senator Kennedy and his wife, Jacqueline, were on the show. A tough act to follow. Listen, R.G., as my father said to me, 'Son, you have the game, but you don't use your head. Don't forget, Bobby Jones is educated. He's a lawyer and a gentleman, and that gives him security. He doesn't get riled, doesn't waste shots.'"

(TAPES ON)
Home golf course. Fifteenth hole. Par four.

I had this guy on the ropes—holed out a niblick on ten, why not? I could hit a sea gull from fifty yards. Then I hooked my drive out there under the branches of a tree. What to do? Chip out on the fairway? Play it safe? Hit a spade mashie to the green? Maybe get lucky. Sink a putt! Or use a low mid-iron . . . hit a bugfucker under the branch, fly the trap, snuggle up . . . birdie time! Drive those idiots crazy! Wow! Still, remember Bobby Jones (the lawyer). Percentage-wise, play it safe.

I went over to my bag, pondering what to do. I looked up, and there was Dad. He had come out to gallery me in. Why did he have to bring his stupid old dog, Duke? He stood there smoking his pipe. I reached for the mid-iron. Our eyes met. I knew what he was thinking. "Play it safe, Son. Remember Bobby Jones."

Of course, etiquette and the rules forbade him to talk to me. Rules, always rules. Rules about everything. Oh, to hell with the rules!

I grabbed the mid-iron, addressed the ball, and hit the little bastard low and true. Dead solid perfect! Then the lousy little dude caught the last twig and jumped in the creek, like it had eyes. I looked back, and there was Dad disappearing over the hill, a disapproving puff of smoke going skyward, Duke at his heels.

I took a seven, birdied the next two holes, went into extra holes, and I finally beat the clown. I beat him, Dad. Rules or no rules!

Dad, why'd you have to leave? Why didn't you follow me in? At least to the clubhouse, Dad. I beat him! All right, screw Bobby Jones. There's always Walter Hagen.

(TAPES CLICK OFF)

"You know, R.G., Walter Hagen was always my idol."

He nodded and asked, "What *about* Walter Hagen?"

I felt drained, weak. "Oh, when I was eighteen—I'll cut it down to one reel—I made it to the State Amateur. The night before, in the clubhouse, smart-ass me had to impress the gathered gentry. Why not? After all, Hagen, the great and immortal 'Haig,' used to show up at the first tee still tipsy, in evening clothes, announcing, 'Which of you guys is going to finish second?' So I had to show them. Him, too. I remember, after about ten Tom Collins's, sleeping on the sofa in the card room. On the first hole, there I stood, eighteen years old, with a massive hangover. Needless to say, my opponent wiped up the course with me."

"Whom did you blame?"

"Walter Hagen. Who else? It was his fault. Screw him. And my father, too! That's when I decided to become an actor."

I could see R.G. was mulling over my convoluted logic. I decided to really impress him.

"I made the cut at the Bing Crosby Tournament just a few years ago. That meant I was privileged to play the final round with Nicklaus, Player, and Palmer!"

He nodded, took a puff on his cheroot, and leaned down to pat his dog, all curled up at his feet.

"Not many of my peers can make that claim. Anyway, to celebrate this great occasion, I toasted myself with one or two Jack Daniels, matching stories with Phil Harris and the boys. A bottle or so later, I made it to my room. I showed up at nine-oh-eight at the first tee. Three thousand people were lining the fairway. Blinding hangover. Then I proceeded to louse up the course. Total disaster!"

"Did you get under any trees?"

"Every tree on the Monterey Peninsula, on national television yet! I remember looking up, and there was Bing, just staring at me. He was smoking his pipe in that cool way of his. Come to think of it, he had a cocker spaniel with him. As I said, he just stared at me. Then he turned on his heel, and he, his dog, and the smoke from his pipe disappeared over the hill."

THIS IS HENNY

I've just been watching Jim practicing drives from the back of our garden, where he hides out from his pals across the road at the Bel-Air Golf Club. He swings that six-iron over and over and over again, trying to hit at least one of his plastic practice balls, generally, to no avail. I can't look very long at this man I adore who, a very short time ago, was one of the best golfers in Hollywood. What am I saying? He'll do it again! I know it! "Come on, Jimmy! Hit it, darling! You can do it! Hey, watch it . . . don't forget, the swimming pool is a hazard, too."

Every year the Los Angeles Police Department holds a golf tournament. Eighty celebrities pair with eighty police officers, best ball of foursome. Proceeds go to widows and orphans of officers killed or wounded in the line of duty. It's a more than worthy cause and a lovely walk in the park. There are lots of impressive trophies for the actors, lots of money for the charity, and a chance to chat and get autographs from their favorites, for the twenty thousand fans and their kids. It's also a chance to see some pretty fair golf.

Jim had played in the police tourney from the time of its inception until his mal set in. Last year, Officer Rudoff called on the very day of the tournament and wanted to know why the hell Jim wasn't playing. I explained that he hadn't played in years. "Put him on, Henny," Rudoff barked. Well, who argues with a cop? "Listen, Jim!" he yelled. "No one wants to see you hack it up. Who cares? They just want to see Mr. Magoo and get his autograph! So I'm sending over a black-and-white, and you just get your ass in it. Over and out!!" "Roger," Jimmy replied, and was on his stumbling way.

Four hours later, he was on the eighteenth hole, 145 yards from the pin, and I was there watching. He had arrived there by a drive that got lucky and bounced off a tree, and a topped second shot that ricocheted off a concrete bridge for a big bounce. Who cares? He actually got there! He was there! He got out of the golf cart, took out his six-iron, and lined up the shot. He glanced skyward at the Deity (so did I), reared back, and hit it. Three years of pent-up adrenalin exploded! That ball took off like a shot out of a cannon. Jim thought it was in. (Later he found out that it had hit the pin and rolled back from the hole.) I couldn't believe my eyes! And the gallery ringing the green went bananas! We exploded with cheers and applause. After a shot like that, it would be heresy to finish the round riding in a cart. (Pop and Duke would never have approved of that.) Jim told me he decided to make it to the green if he had to crawl. He set off on that 145 yards to home with the cheers and applause building and building. As he lurched onto the eighteenth green, the gallery—two hundred strong—rose from the grass and stood. I know that that moment must have been sweeter to Jimmy than if he had won the Masters and the Open rolled into one!

THIS IS JIM

P.S.   I missed the putt.

11

The Karen Horney Syndrome*

WHEN DR. PARKINSON came up with his charming malaise, he didn't miss a trick. They really ought to rename it "Catch 22." Just when you have one element contained, another little dandy rears its catastrophic head. You can't win for losing.

As I said in a previous chapter, I purposely have done no research. I'm just trying to tell it as it happened to me, or, more to the point, as it *is* happening to me.

The main thing is exercise, exercise, and more exercise. That plus ever-increasing doses of L-Dopa, till the dosage and the need cancel each other out. That happy plateau, that Nirvana, at which point they (who "they" are has never been explained) have found out the correct amount of the drug your body requires is the amount you receive until you go to that great telethon in the sky.

As anyone connected with Parkinson's is sure to say, "You don't die from it, you die with it." (Yak, yak!) A sure-fire boffo! A showstopper!

---

*Karen Horney: The first prominent lady psychoanalyst, who, when asked about the rigors of her profession, uttered that now-famous old saw, "Who listens?" One-half of that celebrated old picture of Freud and Horney—Freud is the one with the beard.

Oh, yes, if you follow instructions, you recover up to 95 percent of what you originally were. The most dedicated of doctors, if asked when that joyous day will arrive, becomes clinically evasive. He prescribes an increase in your dosage and departs on a long sea voyage. (At one point, the three doctors handling my case were off—one was in South America rounding the Horn, one was in Hawaii curling ten, and the third was shooting the white waters of the Colorado River in a rubber bedpan. But *my* exchange was in touch with *their* exchange.)

It is a well-documented fact (I think I mentioned it earlier on) that L-Dopa arouses you sexually. This I took with a grain of saltpeter. What I didn't know was that among the pill-heads, the dope-smokers, the hot-tub-addicts, the sex-groupies, the anything-for-a-kick set, L-Dopa is a going item. It's somewhere between cocaine and poppers. Its street worth is five dollars a pill, and here I am with a drawerful. Come to think of it, I could sell them and open my own auto factory—not a DeLorean, a Backus!

Here I was, walking around with a monkey on my back and didn't know it! When it comes to narcotics, I'm completely naive. Sure, I've smoked grass, pot, or shit, as it was so charmingly called during my "prairie" years. I smoked it when you could go to the slammer for one-to-five! I don't smoke it now because I gave up smoking, and what I really crave is a Winston or a Pall Mall. Besides, pot never did anything to me or for me.

At a party given by one of the town's most affluent hedonistic hosts, I was passed some white powder on a silver tray. Thinking it was some kind of canapé, I proceeded to spread it on a tiny cracker, which I promptly wolfed down. I had just devoured an hors d'oeuvre with a street value of two thousand dollars! Needless to say, I have never been asked back by my caftaned host.

As for L-Dopa being a sexual stimulant, bah humbug! As far as I am concerned, as an aphrodisiac, it's on a par with a Nelson Eddy-Jeanette MacDonald musical! It's as sensual as a Pillsbury Bake-Off; as erotic as the locker room of the DAR. Sure, I have lust in my heart. I fantasize being turned out to pasture to graze with the Dallas Cowgirls. I have fallen for all the hoopla—the ginseng root and ground-up rhino horn; what's more, I went hook, line, and sinker for the one about seafood. They told me oysters were surefire; that they never miss! so I ate a dozen, but only seven worked. Then I tried a pill that was so strong, unless I swallowed it fast, I got a stiff neck! I remember fondly that a hangover used to fuel my libido.

(TAPE ON)
(X-RATED)
Sunday morning. Pursuing Henny from room to room like the center-fold of the *Kuma Satra,* climaxing on the pool table, and racking up the score with a cue.
(TAPES CLICK OFF)

Again without warning, Dr. Parkinson tapped me with his wand. I was inadvertently watching "The Lawrence Welk Show" when it struck with all the force of a soggy pizza—a slight stirring in my knickers, a mild swelling in my Fruit of the Loom jockey shorts! So this was the L-Dopa-induced satyriasis I had heard so much about. Big deal! Where was the clap of thunder, Venus emerging from a bearded clam, Zeus zeroing in on a covey of pink-and-white milkmaids, Leda balling her well-hung swan, or even Milton Berle chasing Aimee Semple McPherson into her organ loft?

For the next few days, I spent most of the time behind furniture trying to hide the evidence of my discomfort. Instead of diminishing, the sensation increased until I was perpetually on the verge of an orgasm. Relief lasted, at best, three to four hours. R.G. was concerned with my plight but felt this was a case for the friendly urologist, "Dr. Goldfinger." After a consultation with Rick, they decided a series of prostatic massages were in order.

For the uninitiated, the prostate is a sneaky, little gland shaped like, and layered like, a clove of garlic. That's the way it was described to me, since I've never seen or met one head on. In layman's terms, it is tucked somewhere between the jewel box and "where the moon don't shine." Its function is shrouded in misty antiquity and cluttered information that has been handed down from generation to generation, all the way down to dirty old men on park benches. After the age of forty, it has a tendency to become enlarged, necessitating massages. These call for a doctor (preferably) to insert his rubber-gloved, petroleum-jelly-covered finger up your rectum while you, the prostatee, are perched doggie-fashion on an examining table. After his finger is inserted, the following bon mot is obligatory, "Doctor, I don't want to find that both of your hands are on my shoulders." At best, it is one of the most undignified, degrading pieces of business known to the world. A good massage is supposedly helpful in pumping up your male potency. But this kind of massage? It's not worth it.

If you ever have to undergo this little ordeal, do it in Beverly Hills, where the medical fraternity makes it as attractive, albeit as expensive, as possible. Listen, any hamlet where its stores won't validate your parking ticket unless you've made a purchase of a thousand dollars or more and where the schools go on location for their class picture can't *ever* be caught with its pants down.

In a Beverly Hills urologist's chambers, you are disrobed and cantilevered into position with your elevated buns, naturally, facing the Bistro Gardens. Then, it's blast-off time! Your modesty is at all times preserved with a succession of Porthault sheets strategically placed, and, if you care to have your X rays retouched, they will put them up to dry right between Gore's and Truman's.

Since my condition is chronic and requires attention at least six times a year, I have been "fingered" all over the world. I never leave home unless I am armed with a letter of introduction from my Beverly Hills urologist to global doctors with whom he has working arrangements.

Once in London, I went to one of his confreres on Harley Street, a "mister" with a much-hyphenated name. Doctors are called "Mister" over there. Don't ask me why. (I'm still working on the lawyer-barrister hang-up, or which one gets to wear the wig.) Anyway, I was ushered into Mr. Much-Hyphenated's ground-floor suite. We were in a lovely room overlooking a little park. It was dominated by a glowing fire and a hissing teakettle. Mr. Much-Hyphenated was a cheerful, portly man dressed in modified morning clothes. We exchanged amenities. Then, after a decent interval, he said, "Shall we?" I assented and waited to be ushered into a clinical cubicle. Nothing! Then it dawned on me. We were about to perform this act of intimacy in this beautiful Georgian drawing room under the autographed photograph of Her Majesty and Prince Philip (at least *he's* Greek!).

I disrobed and hung my clothes on the tea hobby and leapt like a trout onto his Chippendale desk, which was complete with a picture of his toothy wife nuzzling a gelding. I assumed the universal position. I was bent over on all fours, my head in the window facing the little park, when I found myself staring eyeball to eyeball with a young lad who was covered with marmalade and clutching a balloon. He was staring right back!

Ah, it was good to be once again on this sceptered isle.

Buns away!

Well, back to Beverly Hills and Dr. Goldfinger. It seems the jock physiotherapist had stretched me too far, thus activating an incipient double hernia, which, in turn, ticked off a dormant prostate gland, which became sensitive to the L-Dopa medication, causing me to go rutting around like a sex-starved water buffalo.

What to do?

Stopping the stretching exercises would cause the Parkinson's to return. Stopping the L-Dopa, which was irritating the prostate, would obviously be disasterous. Surgery at this time, with my Parkinson's, was out of the question. Surgery for the hernia was impossible unless the prostate situation was remedied first. Talk about Catch 22!

Meanwhile, a crazed, ruptured Parky on the constant edge of ejaculation was roaming the streets of Beverly Hills. Mind you, the trouble with the prostate was nothing new. I had had it, chronically, for years. I had once undergone minor exploratory surgery on the offending appendage. They let me see the X rays. My prostate looked like W. C. Fields' nose.

While the medics were pondering the options, I was in a rather agitated state, rubbing up against fire hydrants, greeting the mailman glassy-eyed, begging the milkman to blow in my ears. It was the most uncomfortable period of my life. Not the most painful, but the most uncomfortable, degrading, frustrating, disgusting period imaginable. I literally crawled the walls. When I tried to explain my symptoms to friends, they would burst into paroxysms of laughter.

"You've been coming for three days?" they would shriek. "Groovy! The most."

I came close to homicide—justifiable!

The worst part was working. Try concentrating on a page of dialogue in front of a camera one flick away from a climax. And that's not counting the embarrassment of what could happen to your wardrobe! The whole thing gives orgasms a bad name!

The fourth agonizing day, the urologist came to my rescue with some new pills. D-i-e-t-h-y-l-s-t-i-l-b-e-s-t-r-o-l. Who can pronounce it? It sounds like a Welsh village or the Polish national anthem. Translated, the pills contain female hormones that rush to the prostate, eliminating the masculine urge. I took this medication twice a day, along with the others. The side effects? Only one. Your nipples enlarge and become tender.

Run for the hills! There's a ruptured Parky with big sore boobs on the loose! Move over Carol Doda!*

---

*Carol Doda is the goddess of topless dancers. She happens to possess two enormous breasts. Her measurement? Forty-four inches—and that's only the one on the left! In her school days, she was the teacher's pet. She could erase the blackboard without leaving her seat. Her act consists of just walking out on the stage and managing to stand up.

12

Roll 'em!

"HEY, JIMBO, WANT to go back to work?"

I recognized the voice. It was Tom, my agent and my good friend. Since "Evaluation Day," he had sensed everything that was going on. He stopped pressuring me to work. He called me at decent intervals, took us to dinner when I was up to it, and phoned every once in a while with flattering offers. (Some that didn't exist.)

"Jimbo, you really should go back to work."

There was a pause.

"Look, it's out at Universal. Only three days. A really stand-out cameo. Money! Guest-star billing!"

Another pause.

"Look, Jimbo, it's not going to get you the Award. It's like the doctor giving the patient an enema, 'Wouldn't help, wouldn't hurt.'"

We often talked in code, tag lines of stories, or shtick.

"I'm thinking. I'm thinking." I do a very good Jack Benny.

"The director wants you very much, and he said to tell you 'No Sweat.' I know how you feel about going back to work—ambivalent." He plunged on, "Like the guy watching his mother-in-law go over a cliff in his new Cadillac."

"Okay, Tom, I'll do it. It'll be a good way to get my feet wet."

"Swell, Jimbo." He sounded relieved. "It doesn't go till next week. I'll phone Jack and tell him when to drive you to wardrobe. Glad you took it."

I was about to hang up.

"And Jim? Listen, I almost forgot. The part is a judge. You can play the whole thing sitting down."

What do you know? Tom had the punch line!

It was that clammy hour just before dawn. The gray fog had rolled in from the sea, shrouding the tree outside my window. I opened one eye and squinted at the bedside clock: 5:30 A.M. Wasn't it always 5:30 A.M. in this ridiculous profession called picture acting? I lay back. It was soft and warm and I had fifteen whole minutes before the alarm went off. Disconnected thoughts and images skittered through my sleep-drugged mind, like so many kites caught in a strong wind. They darted capriciously this way and that. I was afloat in space.

(TAPES CLICK ON)

I had made my first stab at being a picture personality for Warner Brothers in a little opera called *One Last Fling* with Alexis Smith. The first day on the picture came clarion clear onto my screen. I drove up to the studio in a spanking-new, bright-red Ford that I had managed to purchase by slipping a hundred dollar bill under the desk of a shady dealer known to all of us as "The Thief of Burbank." To have a car, a *new* car and so soon after the war. Bliss!

The studio guard consulted his clipboard and stuck a friendly face into the window.

"Good morning, Mr. Backus. You're to go to makeup, then the Second Assistant will take you to Stage 14." He stuck his head in farther and grinned at me. You're new, aren't you?"

I nodded.

"When they ran your test," he continued, "I hear one Warner turned to the other Warner and said, "Oh, brother!"

He doubled over with laughter, then waved me through the gate like I was a real movie star. How I wished Henny could be there to share this moment with me. Camelot! If I could only bronze it, I thought. Freeze it in time!

Eight years later.

Same gate. Same cop.

"Hi, Scotty."

"Hi, Jim. Good to have you back at Warner's."

"Good to be back. That Metro's a factory."

"They're still serving that Louis B. Mayer matzoh ball soup in the commissary?"

"Every day at lunch. Best thing on the menu."

He stuck his head in the window and looked around conspiratorially. "Tell me something, Jim. Does it hurt the matzohs when they cut off the balls?" He laughed uncontrollably.

It was the same. Only the car was different, a blue Oldsmobile convertible. I didn't listen when I was advised to spend the three hundred extra and get a Cadillac. "People will think you wanted one but came up short," they warned me. Hollywood logic.

The cop consulted his clipboard.

"*Rebel Without a Cause.* You're on Stage 14. They'll make you up in your dressing room. That new Second Assistant wanted you to go to the Makeup Department. He's a real pain in the ass!"

Two years later.

Same gate. Same cop.

Again the car was different. A black Cadillac convertible a block long. A black car. That's cool! It shows that you don't give a damn whether it rains and spots your car or not! More Hollywood logic.

"Hi, Scotty."

"Hi, Jim, how are things over at Fox? Hey," he stuck his head in the window, "did you hear the new one about the extra girl? She works at Metro by day and Fox at night."

I drove through and left him to his laughing.

(TAPES CLICK OFF)

I lay back, savoring the memories. I wanted to stretch them out, float with them. Time was on hold. There was no Parkinson's back then in those waning precious days. God! To be able to remake those tapes. Do them all over again and wring out every golden ounce.

Good ol' Scotty and his corny jokes.

I had one for him for a change. "What are two homosexuals named 'Bob' called? Oral Roberts! Come on, Scotty, it's all in the delivery. You've got to hit the Oral, or there's no joke!"

What was the matter with me? There was no Scotty anymore. He'd been replaced by a plastic disk you inserted into an automatic candy-striped gate. They even changed the name of the Warner Brothers Studio. They renamed it the Burbank Studios. There goes the "they" again. Who the hell were "they?" All I know is "they" were out to get us. Imagine changing the name of Warner Brothers to Burbank Studios. Warner's was the turf of legends! Or better still, legends about legends. Humphrey Bogart—couldn't punch his way out of a paper bag. Edward G. Robinson—always winced and closed his eyes when he fired his roscoe. And, according to an independent lavatory test, Errol Flynn was a lousy lay.

Warner Brothers—once the spawning ground of Presidents. Now Burbank—spawning ground of "Fantasy Island."

What next? The Vatican Hilton? Let's get a reservation on the Sistine roof. Two Michelangelo Collins's and you're flat on your back looking at the ceiling. "Here's paint in your eye!" Or how about two Bloody Mary Magdalenes? Two Bloody Mary Magdalenes and you're stoned!

What the hell. At least I had a glimpse of it when it was great. When it was a movie studio where sometimes a great movie was made like *Treasure of the Sierra Madre* or *Sergeant York* or the never-to-be-forgotten, romantic *Casablanca*.

These, incidentally, are a far cry from the kind of movies they make at that little studio where I have kept an office for the past ten years. They make mostly commercials at Carthay Studios, including mine, and an occasional cheapie horror movie, plus a great many tit-and-sand epics. I was sitting in my office the other day thinking about how different it was when I was young and getting started.

(TAPES CLICK ON)

I thought back to my very first job: an eighty-year-old Hassidic rabbi in a production of *The Dybbuk* at the Cleveland Playhouse, one of the earliest prestigious regional companies.

I was seventeen years old and treading water until time to enter the American Academy of Dramatic Arts in the fall and then become a Broadway star and a famous matinee idol (typical seventeen-year-old confidence). I phoned the Playhouse and told them I was James Gilmore Backus and that I was going on to Broadway in a few months but would be willing to appear in their current production. The man patiently explained that they were doing a production of a famous Yiddish classic called *The Dybbuk* and the only parts open were for very old rabbis. I allayed his doubts by assuring him that I was a master dialectician with a repertoire of "Two Black Crows," "Cohen on the Telphone" and a fabulous imitation of Lionel Barrymore that might be a good offbeat way of playing a rabbi. He thanked me, but . . . "No."

I discussed it with my grandmother, "Wa Wa," who gave me some swell pointers. She wasn't sure what rabbis were, but she thought they were something like Reverends, so why not play it like Father Coughlin.

I called the Playhouse again the next day, and, thanks to Wa Wa's coaching, told them once again that I was James Gilmore Backus and that my sister was Mrs. Marcus Alonzo Hanna III, whose family owned the Hanna Theater, the Hanna Building, the Hanna Steamship Line, and The Cleveland News, as a tax write-off. I went on to explain that this would almost guarantee glowing notices. The director was very nice but felt I was too young, and, anyway, the rabbis had very few lines. They mostly chanted. Gee, what luck, I thought. Maybe Bing Crosby and Perry Como started that way, only *they* called it crooning.

I consulted my parents that night. Mother suggested I play the rabbi like that man in *Rain*. "After all, he was a preacher, too." My father explained about "some of his best friends" and thought I should play it safe and do it like the Mad Russian on "The Eddie Cantor Show."

The next day, I went to the Playhouse in person. I ambled in wearing my understated Brooks Brothers suit, my snap-brim hat, and my white bucks. They were impressed, but, even though I told them that with my family and connections there wouldn't be an empty seat in the house, they still wouldn't buy it. I pleaded that I *had* to get this part because I didn't believe in nepotism and I wanted to be independent.

The director argued that even with a beard I wouldn't quite make it, though, he assured me, they really wanted me. So I solved their problem with something I remembered from Comparative Religions: one of the oldest Judaic cultures is in Ethiopia; therefore, I could play it in blackface and use my "Kingfish" voice. Selah!

Somehow I got the part. I must confess, I never made it to the opening night. Dirty politics from within. Professional jealousy! They must have found out I wasn't circumcised, even though I was willing to undergo a minituck!

(TAPES CLICK OFF)

A knock on my office door rudely brought me back. In came a kid I thought had everything going for him. Looks, style, and raw talent. I had tried to help him by calling a few people. I hadn't seen him in a good six months. He was grinning from ear to ear.

"Hi, Trip." I was pleased to see him. "According to your face, you're working."

"Yup," he smiled broadly, "I finally broke the ice. Got a good one. Two-week guarantee!" Bambi makes a buck. Then he started to tell me about it. As I listened, I became more and more horrified.

"But, Trip," I exploded, "that's a dirty movie! It's pornography! Don't you know that?"

"Sure," he nodded, "I know it."

"But that's a hard-core porno film," I yelled. "Don't you understand what that means? It means you'll never get a real part in this town. Not after they've seen you in a thing like that!"

"Oh," said Trip blowing it off, "they're never going to see me."

"Never going to see you? What do you mean? You're in it, aren't you?"

"Sure," he said patiently. "But they'll never actually see me because, you see, I'm the standby hard-on!"

Actors! God bless them. They're wonderful. Go on, kid. Be the standby hard-on and, when you're up there getting the Academy Award for "Best Performance by an Actor," I won't tell. I'll never tell. I promise.

I rolled over. It was 5:30 A.M. The alarm went off right on cue. And then I heard footsteps. It was Jack, on his way up the stairs to help me get dressed. As we Parky's say, "One shoe at a time."

13

The X-Rated Magoo

I WAS TAKING a nap when the phone rang. It was the U.P.A. people, producers of *Mr. Magoo*. They were very excited about a whole new concept for the character. The "Today" show was interested in Mr. Magoo's comments on the political scene on a daily basis. What an annuity! After thirty-one years of being the alter ego of the myopic little curmudgeon, this was a piece of cake!

But wait a minute! I couldn't do that. I had Parkinson's disease. It was affecting my speech now, and I could no longer project. Sometimes you couldn't understand me, and I couldn't be heard. The carrot was being dangled in front of my nose, and here I was hobbling around barely able to make it across the room. It was because Henny insisted that I agreed to do it. "You've *got* to!" She told me, "You'll never forgive yourself if you don't!"

I let her take care of the whole thing and went back to my nap.

(TAPES ON)
NBC Studios. "Hollywood Squares." 1975.

Peter Marshall was asking the question, "Whose is the second most identifiable voice in the world?"

The contestant looked us over and chose me. As a gag, I answered,

"Mr. Magoo," intending to immediately add, "No, no, I'm only kidding. It's really Mae West."

But I was right. Mr. Magoo *is* the second most identifiable voice in the world. The contestant agreed with me and won. The audience went wild, and I couldn't have been more flattered.

Then the question was raised if Mr. Magoo was the second most identifiable voice in the world, who was the *first?* They had an answer for that one, too. Guess. Mickey Mouse? Churchill? W. C. Fields? No! Wrong! The most identifiable voice in the entire world is that of an unknown imam, whose voice *on tape* calls the entire Moslem world to prayer. Think about it. In 1970, in India alone he had an audience of more than 875 million people. That's a huge share of the Neilson rating.

(TAPES CLICK OFF)

The thought of doing Magoo again terrified me. All systems were not "go." All systems were gone. My day began to curl at the edges.

Where did I get the little character, anyway? It was so long ago. I thought about it. Radio! Was that where he started? Funny, I had almost forgotten. Back in the golden days of radio, I used to do twenty- to twenty-five shows a week. It was easy. After all, we didn't have to learn lines; we had no costume changes or makeup; no moves on a stage. All we had to do was show up on time and read off a piece of paper.

We raced from one studio to another all day long.

We would run into the studio and do a rough reading for a "timing." This ran about eight minutes for a fifteen-minute show. The rest of the show was the opening and closing, the hefty half-way commercial, and then a little plug at the end. Because the advertiser was getting a free ride, it was called a "hitch hike." After the rough reading, we did another one, this time around the mike, with all the sound effects. It was laughingly referred to as the "dress rehearsal." Then "Airtime!" The actual broadcast.

We finished, got our money, got the hell out, and ran like mad to do the next show. Total time, portal to portal, one hour. Total salary, $21.00. Union scale. Granted, the money was a little tired, but I did do two or three of those every day, plus several commercials, and at least one big comedy or dramatic show each night (union scale, $115.00). And let's not forget that in those days, for example, a dinner for two at 21 or The Stork Club, with a bottle of wine, came to five bucks plus the tip.

At one time, I was doing three soap operas every day. One was a running part on "Stella Dallas" playing her wealthy, haughty son-in-law, Dick Grosvenor. The role of Dick Grosvenor had also been played by Gregory Peck, Barry Sullivan, Dane Clark, Frank Lovejoy, Richard Widmark, and Everett Sloane, to name but a few. The part was fun, as I had the pleasure of throwing the cloying Stella Dallas out on her ass in every episode.

The producers had us over a barrel. Anytime we wanted a raise, they would fire us and get another Dick Grosvenor. Who could tell? It was radio.

Another thing they did was to make us do what was called an AFRA (American Federation of Radio Artists) double. In addition to our regular part, we were required to throw in, gratis, another character, a voice as far removed from our natural one as possible. It was just part of a working actor's repertoire. Everybody did it. It was very important that we sounded different in the second character, as we often had to play scenes with ourselves—electronic masturbation.

On the Fred Allen show, I had enlarged my double into a more dimensional character. We even gave him a name, Fred F. Kelcey, president of Kelcey's Nuts and Bolts. You know the type. The kind of a guy who introduces himself to you, presents his lodge identification and business credentials, and proceeds to tell you jokes you've already heard, laughing right through the punch line. This loud-mouthed prototype showed up in most of the big-time comedy shows, finally settling in as a regular with Edgar Bergen, and I wound up as the AFRA double for my AFRA double.

About this time, a group of dedicated, fiercely creative artists had broken away from Disney and formed United Productions of America. They had had a tremendous success with their first little cartoon, *Gerald McBoing Boing,* and were now getting ready to do a new one about a very near-sighted, nettlesome, old party who takes his banjo-playing nephew, Waldo, on a vacation to the mountains, En route, the fur-coated Waldo falls out of the car and a bear falls in. The rest of the short is the nephew climbing back into the car and ousting the bear, and vice versa. Since they're both wearing fur coats, the near-sighted uncle thinks they are one and the same. Good old mistaken identity. Good enough for Shakespeare—good enough for us.

Jerry Hausner, who later directed the cartoons, remembered my doing Fred Kelcey on radio and suggested me for the part. I went over to UPA, looked at the storyboard, laughed at the drawings of the little man, read the dialogue, ad libbed a little, and it was love at first sight.

THIS IS HENNY

Most people think a cartoon is made by the actor's dubbing his voice to the picture. Not so. Not in Jim's case, anyway. Jimmy was always shown a storyboard. A storyboard is a series of rough sketches with suggested dialogue printed below. John Hubley, the creator, would explain his idea for the story and leave the rest up to Jim. The picture was then animated to Jim's recorded voice. This is how the Magoo cartoons that first swept the country and were heralded as works of art were made. I can proudly say that 50 percent of the dialogue consisted of Jim's ad libs and catch phrases. They used to make three sound tracks, one for the company, a slightly blue one for Hubley, and an all-out, no-holds-barred one for Jim. Hubley would then cull from all three. If you take one of the vintage films and run it in the quiet of a projection room, underneath all the mumbles you will hear political comments, names of our friends, tag lines of dirty jokes, and, occasionally, a barrage of Anglo-Saxon expletives worthy of a Henry Miller. In one Oscar-winning episode, a sexy girl phones Magoo and asks him to babysit, and throughout her dialogue, Magoo is muttering what he would like to do to her. Somehow, it never occurred to anyone to censor a Magoo cartoon.

Magoo, according to Jim, is a raunchy, lecherous, ultra-conservative, mildly racist, skirt-chasing, old bastard. We've always felt that an X-rated Magoo done with a bit of taste would be a blockbuster. Can you imagine that nearsighted old curmudgeon mistaking a house of ill repute for a car wash? Or a gay disco for the Union Club? How about a monster picture, like *Magoo Meets the Transvestite Who Ate New York.*

The little cartoon became an instant smash. They named the character Mr. Magoo, Quincey Magoo, Rutgers-Naught One, and went on to make the series. That was thirty-one years ago. It's still going strong.

THIS IS JIM

I decided to take a nice Rip Van Winkle nap and forget the whole thing.

The darn tapes kept clicking on and off.

(TAPES ON)

London going absolutely mad over Magoo.

The picture someone sent me of a marquee: "*Mr. Magoo* cartoon. Also, *Lawrence of Arabia.*"

Theaters running no other movies—just Magoos, one after the other.

The headline the first time I ever went to England: "Princess Margaret's true love arrives in London. Mr. Magoo is here in person."

We certainly had a hit, but what about the pressure groups. We were making fun of a handicapped person. In more than a million letters, we only got a handful of complaints. My humble diagnosis? People sense that Magoo can see better than any of us. What's more, he sees exactly what he wants to see. Magoo is universal. Everyone can identify with him. There is one in every family, every factory, every army camp. He doesn't necessarily have to be nearsighted. In England, he's John Bull.

My friend Quincey (Magoo), won the Academy Award in 1954. He won it again the next year, 1955. I wasn't invited to accept the Oscar, and my nearsighted little friend never even asked me to the party.

(TAPES FADE OFF)

The fatal morning came, dull, leaden, uncompromising. I couldn't imagine facing it. Parkys are all alike, retreating, procrastinating, fearful of being with other people. We know it, but knowing doesn't help a bit. If we know our fears are groundless, they therefore do not exist. Right? Wrong! "Psychosomatic," Rick had said. He had explained it to me. We had intellectualized it together.

Still I lay there cowering. One more hour and Jack was to drive me to the recording studio. To do what? A lousy little Magoo! Why was I shaky? I used to do Magoo's in my sleep. I could phone them in! Now I lay panicked, numb with fright, like a neophite going for his first audition! Snap out of it. Come on, damn it! You've opened on Broadway! The big time, Las Vegas! Played to 30 millions at one crack on television.

I pulled a pillow over my head and burrowed into the bed.

The trip to the studio was tumbrel time. I kept praying for an accident. A little one. Nothing serious. Little headlines: "Actor injured in crash. Not hurt much. Hospitalized for observation." No way! Jack was driving like Mario Andretti.

"I talked to Hank Saperstein," Jack said as we drove along. "He says that today they're going to do five Magoo comedy news spots for the

"Today" show. One is a song. Then you, straight, as yourself, Jim Backus, for the introduction."

He must have sensed my panic.

"Don't worry, Jim. I know you're a bit shaky, so I told them you were just getting over the flu. You won't have to stand at the mike. They rigged up an easy chair for you and a music stand beside it for your script."

I looked at Jack like a grateful calf.

An hour later, we were headed back home. It was over! Done! How, I'll never know. I simply don't remember. Technique over terror, I guess.

"You see, I told you it was a cinch," Jack volunteered.

"Yeah, the chair and the music stand did the trick."

There was a long pause.

"Jim, you never used that chair or the music stand. Not once!"

"Never used the chair?"

"As Magoo, no. You were jumping all over the place, and, boy, can you sing! Funny thing, though, when you were yourself, Jim Backus, doing the intros, then you *did* sit in the chair! I mean, you were so weak," he continued, "we could hardly hear you. Your voice went. They had to jack up the sound."

It *was* a funny thing. Funny? It was weird. And as for the song, I can't sing at all. I have a tin ear, but how come as Magoo, I could sing? That's crazy, I thought to myself. Jim Backus and Mr. Magoo are one and the same person—or are they?

14

C'monna My House

WE WERE GIVING a party. It was our first one in three years, or was it four? God, it was good to see so many loving, caring friends again. They all stopped by my cushioned chair for a kiss. The evening was highlighted by a surprise visit from Richard Burton. Our friendship had been cemented by three months together on an Alaskan location for the movie *Ice Palace.*

THIS IS HENNY

So close were we, in fact, that Richard, Jimmy, and I became a threesome around town. Once, while we were listening to Don Rickles insult the customers during one of his nightclub appearances, Don spotted us in the audience and said, "There they are again! Richard Burton and Jim and Henny Backus! And you wanna know something? Henny's the 'beard!'"*

Several years after the completion of *Ice Palace,* I went along with Jim on a personal appearance tour. When we hit Boston, Richard was there,

---

*"Beard": Example: You are a married man having an affair with a lady who keeps nagging you to take her out. You finally agree, but only if your friend can come along. Your pal and your girl behave as though they are the daters. He saves your face, hence, he is a "beard."

too, with *Camelot,* which was being tried out prior to its Broadway opening. We made a date to meet for dinner at the Ritz-Carlton Hotel.

The Boston Ritz is conservative, quiet, and elegant. Richard and I, ever the punctual ones, were there at 7:00 sharp. Naturally, Jim was late. We were having a drink, and the conversation spilled over, with both of us laughing and talking at once. This caused some raised eyebrows and a few shushes. Animated conversation is not tolerated at the Ritz!

Suddenly, we spotted Jimmy standing in the doorway. He and Richard saw each other at the same time. I must digress right here for a moment and tell you one thing about actors. They are very effusive people, who hug and kiss each other, regardless of sex, with great abandon. Hulking male stars greet each other with, "Hello, darling!" "Nice to see you, sweetie!" "See you later, lover!" Let me tell you, my husband has called John Wayne pet names he never even called ME on our wedding night!

Well, naturally, Jim and Richard rushed to embrace, and just as they were about to fall into each other's arms, Richard shot a glance around the disapproving room and whispered, "Not on the lips! This is Boston!"

THIS IS JIM

As the party jelled, people gathered in knots in the den. Our den is the smallest room in the house, yet sixty or more people will crowd in there or the adjoining bar, ignoring the rather spacious living room, not to mention the tented-over terrace, which not one guest has ever graced. People love to be jammed together at parties, I guess. The conversation bubbled like the champagne they were drinking.

As I awkwardly made my way from group to group, I realized that people had to explain to me what was currently going on, what deals were being made, what picture had been shut down, and what were the latest network shenanigans. I fared no better at conversation with the ladies, or with the cadre of comics. I felt as *au courant* as a drawing on the wall of a cave. Even the cummerbund on my dinner jacket struck a discordant note. I looked like something out of Xavier Cugat's rhythm section. I retreated to the sanctity of my pillow-padded chair.

A few of the old guard stayed on for a nightcap. Soon they, too, left in a covey of Corniches.

I sat before the fire and tried to remember my last picture. Was it three years ago? Was it four? Who cares! I couldn't even remember the title.

(TAPES ON)

I did remember, though, that I had played the part of a Texas fascist who had a ragtag army of fanatics bivouacked on a deserted ranch. We were being stalked by three young ladies from the CIA: one, an amazonian WASP; one, a leonine black lady; and one, a hybrid Oriental. Each was dressed in black leather, thigh-high boots, a G-string, and a bandolier larded with a Baretta and other James Bond accoutrement, suggesting an overlay of sadomasochism.* They were nude from the waist up, and, since they all possessed alarming dimensions, they made an imposing trio.

We were shooting this epic on the old Paramount Ranch outside the town of Agoura. "MASH" used the same facility, which should give you some idea of the ruggedness of the terrain. The temperature was hovering around the freezing point.**

One scene called for a fight between my militia and the three avenging ladies. The action ended with their dumping a vat of spaghetti over my head. There I was at one o'clock in the morning with ice cold marinara sauce oozing down my medals. What to do? I had one hour off, so I commandeered a jeep and headed for a lone bar eight miles down the road for a drink. On my way, I spotted the dark lady shivering in the semidarkness as she tried to get the key into the lock of her portable dressing room door. I asked her if she would care to join me in a jar of warming brandy, and since she, too, had an hour's respite, she acquiesced. We were off! Ten minutes later, we entered the Prairie Oyster and marched to the bar. In my best macho tones, I commanded, "Two double brandies!"

The bartender looked up from putting his glasses and olives in numerical order and, for the first time, saw a general wearing riding boots and a Patton field jacket, with side arms, a Rommel-style cap, and tank goggles. He also saw, flanking the general, a black amazon with a

---

*Sadomasochism: First credited to the Marquis de Sade, who indulged in same from the time he was a little whippersnapper. Hollywood version: Putting male partner in bondage. He is then talked down to, ordered about, humiliated, debased, degraded, and denied sexual release . . . not unlike a Beverly Hills marriage.

**Freezing point: It is alleged that cold weather makes a woman's nipples stand out. True! This explains why, whenever you see a picture of an Eskimo, he is always smiling.

carbine slung across her bare chest and an ominous Baretta protruding from her navel.

The bartender was dumbfounded. He was speechless. He just stood there. After a sufficient pause, I rapped on the bar with my field marshal's baton and barked, "What's the matter? Don't you serve members of the armed forces?"

That's the way it was three years ago, or was it four? Oddly enough, the same thing happened to me twenty-five years ago when Victor Mature and I were playing Centurion and Captain in George Bernard Shaw's *Androcles and the Lion.*

Which reminds me, with us in *Androcles* was that true actor's actor, that darling man, the late Robert Newton. I know you remember him, Bobby of the rolling eyes and the rollicking voice intoning, "God love you, Matey!" It seems that Mr. Newton had a lock on pirate parts, but in *Androcles,* Bobby was playing the part of Ferovious, the giant slave with a heart of gold who embraced Christianity with maniacal fervor. It was no secret that Mr. Newton was fond of the drink, and stories of his bouts with booze are legendary. In *Androcles,* he rode on a scrawny little burro and had developed a great fondness for the beast. It was always with him, and after a day of shooting he would leave the studio, taking his new-found friend along to all of his haunts. He used to say with great glee, "I am the first man to show his ass in the lobby of the Beverly Hills Hotel!"

When Bobby, Vic Mature, and I were making Howard Hughes' production of *Androcles and the Lion,* most of the shooting time (long days of it) were spent in filming scenes of the Roman soldiers herding Christian slaves to be thrown to the lions in the Colosseum.

(The Colosseum stage manager used to call, "Martyrs, five minutes, please!")

There were huge caravans of slaves and livestock constantly being poked and prodded into position past the cameras. At one time on this movie, we had an enormous procession of Roman soldiers, Christian martyrs, horses, donkeys, and elephants. Since this journey took us through the Italian countryside en route to Rome, we passed happy peasants, who were invariably herding sheep or geese. Sheep, fine! But I was playing a Roman officer, and part of my costume was a leather armor micro-mini skirt. So, I had to wear body makeup, and at five-thirty in the morning! The makeup man with that cold sponge (I think!?)—it could have been a tall dog! I learned very early that a trip through a gaggle of geese was an invitation to gang molestation, and a quick understanding of the derivation of the word, "goosed."

One of the main reasons for all the delays on this Howard Hughes holocaust was that every time they finally got all the people and animals in line and ready to shoot, one of our four-footed thespians would become visibly sexually aroused, and we would be sent to our trailers to wait till the wranglers (animal handlers) would hose down our horny background players. Actually, there was much more carrying-on right on the set than in the dressing rooms. It was estimated that the barnyard peccadillos were costing Mr. Hughes more than his own little didoes at the Beverly Hills Hotel.

Anyway, Vic and Bobby Newton, and I were sitting in Vic's digs, and the subject of ladies came up. Vic, who loved to hear Bobby sound off in his beautiful voice, had the ability to put him "on" without Bobby ever being aware of it. So he did. . . .

"Bobby, you've been all over the world. Which ladies appeal to you the most?"

"Oh, Matey, I love them all, their roundness and their softness, all shapes and sizes and colors. I shall never forget a Ubangi lass. Lovely! She used to slip her lips under the door, and I'd sneak a good night kiss."

"Now, Bobby, you're copping out. I mean, if you had to make a choice. Just one, no more."

"Well, my Hearty, and you, Jim, it would be the Irish coleens."

"Why is that?"

"Well, I was making a picture in Ireland and rather than stay at the local hotel with the rest of the company, I was boarding in a little cottage, thatched roof and all, by the sea. I took quarters under the eaves— shared a room with some doves. I lived with this delightful family, the Malones, the farmer father, the bountiful mother, and their three beautiful daughters, Mavoureen, Bridget, and Molly.

"One evening I was coming home at dusk, and I spotted Mavoureen, all of sixteen, with those flashing green eyes, climbing over a stile. Well, the sight of that pink flesh peeking out of her petticoat was enough to drive a man daft. So I grabbed her and kissed her and threw her in the peat bog and had my way with her, while the rabbits scurried out of the heather. It was glorious!

"Two days later I was coming home by way of the seashore, and there, gathering cockels and mussells, was Molly Malone. She had tucked her skirt up under her bodice, and the sight of those ivory thighs, like two ionic columns, was like heady ale. So, I just took her in my arms and threw her in a kelp bed, and the waves washed over my bare buttocks, and the seals beat their flippers in time to my mighty thrusts."

We were rapt. There was a pause, and Vic said, "Go on, Bobby. There must be more!"

"Well, Matey, and you, too, Jim, the next evening I went to the barn to learn my lines, and there, sitting on a stool, was Bridget, milking a cow. As I towered over her, the sight of her breasts like two ripe melons drove me into a frenzy, so I took her in my arms and threw her in the hayloft and had my way, while the chickens cackled and the cows lowed and rang their bells.

"Two nights later, we did night shots and at 3:00 A.M. I wended my way to that cottage-by-the-sea, and, much to my surprise, Sheilagh, the Junoesque mother of the three lovely maids, was waiting up to give me tea. The thought of this two-hundred-pound, wanton matron was too much! So I kissed her and threw her on the hearth, and while I mounted this Mother of Creation, the coals crackled and the kettle hissed a merry tune. I loved them all, every member of that Malone family!"

We were both terribly impressed with Mr. Newton's glorious delivery and the lyrical details of his amorous encounters. Vic thought for a while, and then he said, "Tell me, Bobby, the truth! Did you ever take a tug on dear old Dad?"

(TAPES OFF)

The tapes came to a feathery stop. I found myself in that delicious alpha state, where dreams and reality are separated by a fine shimmering line. I was aware that the fire had burned down to dying embers. I could feel the champagne lapping at my damaged basal ganglion.* Something new they told me I had that day, a week or so ago, when they decided to take me off L-Dopa and try a new drug, a mood elevator called Nardil.

I welcomed the new tapes that suddenly appeared. Vignettes skittered across my screen: *Mad, Mad, Mad, Mad, World*—two weeks without letup in the mock-up of a tiny Cessna two-seater. Two weeks in that fake

---

*Basal ganglion: A nerve of the motor system that transmits messages from the brain to other ganglia. A malfunction which causes the patient to do bad imitations of Jerry Lewis. (From the Latin "ganglia-banglia.")

space capsule with Mickey Rooney and Buddy Hackett. Two weeks in a flying egg crate, suspended forty feet up. Two weeks with no air! To simulate turbulance, the director, Stanley Kramer, had to spin the damned thing at 360°, causing us to richochet off the walls and ceiling like so many Ping Pong balls. "Keno, anyone?"

(TAPES ROLLING ON)

Location: training camp for a fight picture in which I played the alcoholic father of a young contender. To show the passage of time, they photographed the pages of a calendar being blown away, one by one, plus the clicking of the wheels of a train, and, finally, a montage of my "boy" in the center of the ring, flailing away at one hapless extra after another. At the moment of inevitable victory, I would leap over the ropes into the ring like a demented stage mother.

To further illustrate the passage of time that my son was spending on fighting his way to the championship, they kept adding things to his face—protruding eyebrows, cauliflower ears, a few welts, and, of course, the ever-popular swollen, bashed-in false nose.

It was common knowledge in our company that our leading man was having a mad affair with the leading lady. This was evidenced at every lunch break by the wild tossing of his flimsy, portable dressing room, the purple expletives emanating from it, and the groans and grunts coming from behind its paper wall, which would have been worthy of an Arnold Swartzenagger pumping iron. During one particularly fervent dalliance, the door flew open. In front of the eighty of us who were lunching on the set, out burst our ingenue, naked as a jaybird, clutching a piece of pink rubber and frantically yelling, "Oh, my God! Oh, my God! It fell off! It fell off!" Suddenly, aware of our presence, she stared down at it again, looked up, smiled, and said, "Oh, it's only his nose!"

(TAPES OFF)

The tapes slithered to a stop. I felt someone's hand. I looked up. It was our man, Johnny.

"Can I help you," he asked. We went up the stairs together. As we slowly reached the top, he smiled at me and said, "A Happy New Year to you, Boss."

15

"Shmuck! Get Away from the Window!"

TONY, MY SHRINK of old, had come back to Los Angeles and taken over my case from R.G. Though R.G. had paved the way, under Tony's tutelage, one after another my physical manifestations left me, only to be replaced by a series of new ones. Why? Was I possessed by a demon? Did I have my own live-in dybbuk? I had a period when I would actually black out if I was confronted by a strange person or a new situation. None of this made any sense at all.

I continued to sink deeper and deeper into a morass of self-pity, even though they upped my Nardil dosage. I had an ungodly fear of life outside my cocoon. I discussed it with Tony, who reiterated that my self-image was deplorable and that I had to stop thinking of all the things I had not accomplished, and concentrate on those that I had. "No more negatives," he scolded. "You gotta ac-cen-tu-ate the positive, ee-lim-i-nate the negative, latch on to the af-firm-a-tive, and *don't* mess with Mr. In-between." Thank you, Johnny Mercer!

(Johnny Mercer, my neighbor, that fey leprechaun and one of the underrated minisingers of our time, has more pungent statements in his lyrics than in the combined works of Freud and Jung.)

Accentuate the positive!

Eliminate the negative!

I was messing with Mister Inbetween. So I wasn't Laurence Olivier—I wasn't even Lawrence of Arabia. They have their own niches, their own bag . . . I have mine.

(FAST TAPE ON)
Playing a round of golf with Ben Hogan and Victor Mature. Hogan, "The Hawk!" Perhaps the greatest golfer of all time. Mature, master or victim of the world's greatest slice. Hogan graciously offered to give Vic a few pointers to rid him of his horrendous banana ball. Vic's reply to the four-time U.S. Open winner, "You stick to your racket, I'll stick to mine."
(TAPE OFF)

Thanks, again, Johnny. His song has ended, but his melody lingers on.

THIS IS HENNY
My husband often forgets that he, Jimmy, has had many honors in his life, like the televised visit from Charles Collingwood on "Person to Person," and the Ralph Edwards surprise on "This is Your Life." He was minding his own business in the Pickwick Book Shop when Ralph Edwards shoved a huge book under his nose and intoned, "JIM BACKUS . . . THIS IS YOUR LIFE!!!," and then proceeded to lead him to a television station where he brought out relatives he hadn't seen in thirty years (and wanted to keep it that way). There was the uncle who sold him an Edsel! And the lady he played doctor with thirty-six years ago. There she stood in her comfortable shoes, her flowered hat, and her surgical stockings at half-mast.

THIS IS JIM
Yes, it's true I've had a few honors.
But the greatest honor of them all was when I became the first person in history ever to go to the bathroom on a Greyhound bus. Was I the first, or could it have been a test pilot from Crane Plumbing?
Now mind you, I'm a bus buff. I'm bus-oriented. It stems from the days when I was a kid doing one-nighters. At that time, a bus stopped every three hundred miles. This was called a "comfort stop." So you see, there's a sort of ESP between buses and me.
Right after the war, like every red-blooded American boy, I came to

Hollywood to be a movie star. In those days I was a starving young actor, and in Hollywood, at that time, they had junkets. This is still going on. A junket is a trip they take you on, all expenses paid, for publicity purposes.

One day, I was sitting at home waiting for the phone to ring, and it did! It wasn't a job. It was the publicity man from the Greyhound Bus Company. He explained that they were inaugurating their new bus, the "Scenicruiser." It was the first time since World War II that they were able to get the materials to make one. The publicity man was trying to round up a group of young actors and starlets to be driven to Palm Springs on this bus, where they would be given lunch and then photographed in "cheesecake" shots in and around the bus.

I figured, what have I got to lose? They said I would be given a free lunch and that there was a bar on the bus and a lady of ample proportions playing an accordian, which could be interesting. Anyway, I had never been to Palm Springs.

So, bright and early the next morning, I boarded the shiny new bus. I was sitting there after having had my prune juice and coffee and reading my morning newspaper. I am a man of very regular habits. Suddenly, I realized, in the back of that bus was a GENTLEMEN'S RETIRING ROOM! So I finished my coffee, took my newspaper, and "retired" thereto. It was the first time there was this convenience on a bus, and I was the first man in recorded history ever to set foot in it. "One giant step for mankind!" I felt just like Neil Armstrong, only his "Men's Room" was strapped to his leg.

At this point, the bus got under way, and so did the public relations man, who took over with his little microphone to describe all of the bus's charms, but I couldn't hear him because I was in the back.

He said, "I want to welcome you aboard the new Greyhound Scenicruiser. Let me point out a few features on this bus that are a FIRST in bus history: our "sceni-deck" up above, where you can relax in air-conditioned comfort and watch the scenery glide by.

"Another first," he continued. "We have a Gentlemen's and a Ladies' Powder Room on this bus, which is definitely another FIRST!" "Now," he continued, "I want to point out a safety feature of this bus—the Westinghouse air brakes. They can literally stop this bus on a dime! Let me see now, there are no cars behind us for about two miles, so I am going to ask the driver to give us a demonstration. We are now going seventy miles an hour, and I am going to ask him to slam on the brakes!"

Now, remember, I couldn't hear him because of where I am with my newspaper . . .

"However," the p.r. man continued, "I must warn you that when he applies the brakes, there will be a tremendous surge forward, so brace yourselves! All clear? Ready? NOW!!"

The brakes were applied, and I shot the whole length of that bus! You think that was embarrassing—how about getting back?

THIS IS HENNY

Jim had another honor almost as special as being the first man ever to go to the bathroom on a Greyhound bus. He was also the first man to scratch himself in an erogenous zone on television. Most of you seem to have forgotten that once upon a time, all television shows were live and never, ever taped. What you saw on your television set was really happening at that very moment. There was no chance of any self-righteous network executive cutting or bleeping anything he might feel was censorable.

This is what happened to Jim one lovely, sunny, spring morning, long long ago, when television was live.

THIS IS JIM

Let me tell you how it happened. We had rented a beautiful Fifth Avenue town house, while I was doing a TV show out of New York. Henny was still in California, and I was alone. The nicest thing about being away from your wife is the fact that you can do any damn thing you please. Not booze and broads. Just rattling around the house with a three-day growth of beard and looking at all the sports shows on the tube and parking the beer can on the rug. Things like that!

I had been up late the night before and was having my first cup of coffee. I sleep in just the tops of my pajamas, so there I was, alone in the house, sitting in the living room with the windows open on that sunny spring afternoon, in the top of my pajamas, drinking my first cup of coffee and doing some early morning scratching. Let's face it. We all do it! There's nothing erotic about it! It's just a general scratching and checking to see that everything is in its proper place. Suddenly, I was aware that something was going on right outside my window on Fifth Avenue. It was a muffled sound, like a parade or something, and it was getting nearer.

This was the year that Dave Garroway did a wonderful show on television called "Wide Wide World." Now, don't forget, "Wide, Wide World" was live! On this particular Sunday, he had chosen to do the story of Fifth Avenue, starting at Washington Square and working his way north. This house, which became the Iranian Embassy, is one of the architectural masterpieces of Fifth Avenue.

Wondering what the noise was all about, I sauntered over to the window, checking and scratching as I went.

The living room had French windows from the ceiling to the floor, and there was just the width of an ordinary sidewalk separating me from Dave Garroway and his entire camera crew. At that time, long distance direct dialing had just become a reality. As I stood there—framed in the window—scratching and arranging and contemplating the red light on Mr. Garroway's camera a mere eight feet away, the telephone rang, and it was Henny from California, who screamed, "SHMUCK! Get away from that window! You're on "Wide Wide World!"

16

Slapstick

IT HAD GOTTEN around in the trade that I was under the weather and therefore unemployable. Good! I settled back in my leather armchair in front of the fireplace and had another cup of tea.

I was unemployable to all but the creator of "Gilligan's Island," a lovely man named Sherwood Schwartz (known to all as Robin Hood's rabbi). He was preparing a two-hour special of our old show and wanted me to join them in my old part of Thurston Howell III. The prospect terrified me. They offered me everything my agent asked for. Late work calls, a limo, anything! They offered me every perk I could think of to thwart them into forgetting the whole thing. I still said "NO." And when, to shake me up, they threatened to write me out and write in a new character, my son, Thurston Howell *IV!*, I was merely relieved. However, I was coerced into showing up in the last scene. I hobbled on looking like death, then retreated into my cocoon. They had found themselves a marvelous new actor named David Ruprecht for the part of my son, and I erased the word "indispensable" from my vocabulary.

Meanwhile, dire reports were printed in two of those scurrilous rags that are on sale in all the supermarkets. One of those publications went so far as to plant men around our house to keep a twenty-four-hour watch. I guess they were waiting for that puff of white smoke.

One day, when I was having a "Why me?" festival, I was interrupted by Nancy, our young secretary. She informed me that there was a lad at the door who insisted on seeing me. "Show him in," I said. I thought I'd regale him with a few anecdotes, some advice, a cup of tea, an autographed picture, and send him packing. It would give him something to tell his grandchildren. What the hell, I had nothing else to do.

In came a young man in denims, a leather jacket, and motorcycle boots, who had just strode out of closet land with a "property." Without further ado, he informed me that his name was Steven Paul, he was twenty-three years old, he had a script by Kurt Vonnegut (unheard of!), a score by Michel Legrand (ridiculous!), had signed Jerry Lewis and Madelene Kahn as the leads (impossible!), plus the amazingly talented comedian, the late Marty Feldman, and a superb character actor named John Abbott, and he was here to sign me to play the President of the United States. (Heresy!) He handed me a script. Still thinking he was some kind of glorified gopher,* I darted like a scalded mouse for the nearest loophole.

"This is all very well, but who's going to produce? And who's going to direct?"

"Oh, I'll be doing both, through my own company."

He then broke another covenant by offering me a decent salary, plus a hefty sum to be paid after the picture was a roaring blockbuster.

"How can it miss?" he asked me. "Vonnegut, Legrand, the new Jerry Lewis, me directing. . . ." He pointed to himself. I nodded weakly. "And you, Mr. President," he added, "the frosting on the cake." He had a point.

He rose and held out his gloved hand.

"Who loves 'ya, baby?"

Hey, this was *real* producer talk! I had trouble rising from my chair and could barely totter to the door.

He stopped. "Looks like you have trouble walking."

"Son," I told him as I struggled to open the door, "there was another President with the same problem."

Nancy stood with me in the doorway. We watched him barrel down the drive. I explained sketchily my encounter with the boy.

---

*Gopher: Someone nepotismatically attached to the company for the purpose of running errands. "Go for coffee." "Go for danish," hence "Gopher." i.e., sometimes compelled to perform lewd acts on the bodies of players important enough to have assigned parking.

"Could be he's nuts!" I said.

"No way," Nancy assured me.

"What makes you so sure?"

"Didn't you see what he was driving? A Mercedes 380SL!"

She had me there.

I realized we were playing with a whole new set of rules.

During the shooting of *Slapstick,* I accomplished another first. I played a scene with two thousand chickens, barnyard variety, of course. Let me digress. In my long and speckled career, I have appeared with tigers, wolves, mice, rats, tarantulas, dogs, horses, camels, gorillas, dolphins, turtles, birds, and oh, yes, lions! When a lion is being used in a picture, extreme safety measures go into effect. The area is cordoned off by guards, and at the door to the sound stage there is always an ominous sign:

DANGER! WILD ANIMALS!
AUTHORIZED PERSONNEL ONLY

One day, I was approaching the stage and read the sign and realized, *I* was an authorized personnel!

Before an episode with a lion is scheduled, each and every woman who is in any way involved with the film (not only actresses, but script girls, makeup girls, wardrobe girls, and others) is discreetly asked—by an assistant director on a bull horn—when she is expecting her period, the presence of which drives the big pussy cats into a frenzy. When our young ingenue was asked whether she had had her menstrual period, she cried, "Yes, thank God!"

I remember on one lion-infested picture, a distinguished fading beauty was asked about *her* cycle. She covered her face with her little liver-spotted hands. Sensing her embarrassment, I said, "I don't blame you for being offended." "Offended!" she replied, "I've never been so flattered in my life." They then asked our character actress whether she had been through menopause.

"Menopause," she cried, "I haven't even been through Disneyland!"

(MGM once had on its cast sheet a call for one million grasshoppers, two vats of crickets to be sprayed green, and a sky full of locusts. Just think of what God could have done if he had had distribution!)

Oddly enough, while working on *Slapstick* with this passenger list from the ark, I was injured only once—and of all things, by a macaw! (Macaws weigh about forty pounds and subsist on a diet of walnuts, which they crack with their razor-sharp beaks.) Since I was to do a scene with this feathered thespian, the trainer suggested that I first win his confidence. I figured the best way to do that, as with any creature, was to feed him, so I hand fed him two sacks of nuts. I was really beginning to gain a meaningful relationship, when suddenly the macaw was seized by some prereptilian trauma and, foregoing the succulent walnuts, sank its beak into the base of my thumb. Six stitches and two tetanus shots later, I returned to the set. Don't ever trust a bird. Not one of them. Not even a gull!

A few weeks later we were on location on Malibu Beach. A member of the cast and I were walking around on the sand waiting to be called for a rehearsal. A flock of birds appeared overhead, and one of them dropped his regards on my friend's head.

"Don't move!" I told him. "I'll get some tissue."

"Don't bother," he replied. "That bird is probably miles away by now!"

My very first shot in the picture was the interior of "Air Force One." It was a mock-up of the real thing. On one side of the plane was the President's desk, his chair, *and* the red phone—the works! On the other side of the aircraft was one continuous wall of chicken crates full of—what else??? Chickens! The plot of *Slapstick* was as follows:

America has lost a nuclear war and has been reduced to a third-rate power. It has no oil whatsoever, and its huge industrial complex is gone. *(Dialogue from film)*

> PRESIDENT (TO YOUNG OFFICER): This once great nation of ours has been reduced to exporting quaaludes, hula hoops, and bumper stickers. "Air Force One," once a symbol of our might, now has to be powered by the only source of energy we have: chicken-shit!

Cut to crates of cackling fowl.
Pan down to ground to a sign:

> Standard Chicken-Shit of New Jersey.

Pan around to another sign:

> Last chicken-shit before the freeway.

This, as I said, was about to be my first shot in the picture. No matter how many times an actor has experienced this, when the assistant director calls, "We're on a bell! Quiet! Roll 'em! ... Ac-SHUN!," it is *something!* It's something you can never explain to anyone who hasn't been there. It really is a terrifying moment. Some actors pray, some make the sign of the cross, some just cross their fingers. The stage-trained actor checks his fly. Most of us sneak one last desperate look at our lines. This is it! Magic time, and you never get used to it. The older *you* get, the worse *it* gets. In his early sixties, Laurence Olivier was stricken with such paralizing stage fright it literally almost killed him.

One critic was so impressed with our "Air Force One" scene, he wrote, "It even has the imperceptable tremor of an airplane." Little did he know, the plane was stationary. The tremor was *me!*

Was it always this way?

(TAPES COME ON)

Rebel Without A Cause. I am playing James Dean's father. We are about to film the first take of a new scene.

> *Interior of a house—night. House is surrounded by teenage hoodlums. They are hiding in bushes and perched in trees. They are trying to lure my son, Jimmy Dean, out of the house by chirping.*
> HOODLUMS *(Suddenly change to hissing)*: Chickie! Chickie! Chickie!

Outraged, I am to storm out of the house via the front door.

ASSISTANT DIRECTOR: Ready, Mr. Backus?

Was I ready? Any time. It's an easy one. What the hell. All I have to do is storm out of the front door and shake my fist at some crazy kids. No sweat! Why, just the day before, I had done a long fight scene where Jimmy Dean threw me down two flights of stairs and across the living room with both of us landing on top of a chair just as it overturned. No doubles! Just one continuous camera move. Was I ready? Just to walk through a front door? "Any time, C.B.!" I yelled.

ASSISTANT DIRECTOR *(Through bullhorn)*: Quiet! Camera rolling!

I stifled a yawn, then gulped in terror. Wait a minute! I had forgotten something. They had mentioned to me, in passing, that to give the scene more of a sense of understated horror, they were going to hang a live chicken on top of the front door, facing me upside down, on a level with my eyes. I didn't have time to really panic.

ASSISTANT DIRECTOR: Speed! Action!

I opened the door and was met by five pounds of enraged fowl right in the kisser, feathers flying! Beak and claws jabbing!

DIRECTOR: Cut! Jim, we're going to have to do it again. It was fine, but you winced. This time, don't close your eyes.

He was right. I had remembered the chicken and anticipated it. The character I was playing would have had no way of knowing that he was going to head into five pounds of flailing fury hanging from the door. My eyes *had* to be open. Try it sometime. What I did is called "Chicken." I guess I am.

(CLICK)

(TAPES OFF)

Slapstick turned out to be a very wild and provocative film. With a script by someone like Kurt Vonnegut, you have to refer to the movie as a "film." Once on a panel show, I called a movie that was being discussed a "movie," which caused Judith Crist to borrow Rex Reed's barf bag.

I managed to get through the picture. I got by with a minimum of difficulty, but the hours were long and some of the scenes very physical and tricky. Once, when I shakily entered the set, I noticed a group of strangers standing around. I was introduced, shook hands, and, still shaking, stumbled over to my chair. It turned out that they were all doctors. They were backing the picture! Can you believe it! And furthermore, they were not only doctors, they were neurologists! That's like a group of Klansmen backing Richard Pryor.

17

"I Gotta Be Me"

DO YOU KNOW those glorious mornings when you wake up and for a fleeting moment you don't know where you are, or who you are, or how you are? Then you *really* wake up with a thundering reality, and it all settles in, and it's you, and you're still sick. Four years of it now. Of what? What was it, anyway? Was it really Parkinson's disease, or wasn't it? Were they lying to me? Holding something back? Did Henny know? Would this panic never lift? Will I ever be me again and not this frightened, shuffling old man? "Make yourself lead a normal life," they kept insisting. "Play a few holes of golf." Golf! Forget it! Pitch and putt maybe—not my kind of golf. I remember golf when I really played it.

(TAPES ON)
Around the big table at the Riviera were Andy Williams, David Wayne, Dean Martin, Donald O'Connor, Bob Wilkie, Pierre Cosette, Jack Carter, Harry Newman, Peter Falk, Karl Kious, Doug Sanders, and Captain Howard Morton: a good group to have on your side, veterans of the French and Indian Wars. Oh, the laughs we had!

"We all play off Doug's ball!"

"Five aside, ten press, twenty-five aggregate!"

"A license to steal!"

"If I get Pierre for a partner, I get an extra shot!"

"Hang by your thumbs, Backus. No extra shot!"

"That Jerry Ford don't play so bad, but oh, those Secret Service guys, clicking their guns on your backswing!"

"Remember Agnew? At Tamarisk, he hit a low slice and caught a guy right in the jewel box. The guy was getting out of his car at the time."

"Balls in the air!"

(TAPES STILL ROLLING)

I remember a game with Captain Howard Morton. Howard was older than we were. He was in his sixties, a senior pilot for American Airlines. He had one hell of a war record. Uncounted treetop missions on D-Day. He was a feisty little bastard, all of five-feet-four, and one hell of a golfer. The captain's wife kept him on a short leash, so out of the rather lucrative senior officer's pay, he got maybe twenty-five bucks allowance. One day he literally wiped up the course with me. He got me for $248.00! He was drooling. $248.00! And all his! While he was salivating, I wrote out a check and handed it to him. He glanced at it and leapt fifteen feet into the air. "This is on a Cleveland bank!" he screamed.

"Calm down, Captain. It's an account I've had since I was a kid. I keep it out of sentiment, and also Henny never knows what I win or lose that way. Sneaky, huh? So take the check—and shut up and buy me a drink."

The next morning a friend of ours took a flight to New York on a 747. Over Chicago, the intercom switched on.

"This is your captain, Howard Morton, speaking. The time is 1:00 P.M. I don't like the looks of the starboard motor."

He clicked off.

Fifteen minutes later the intercom clicked on again.

"This is your captain speaking. I really don't like the looks of the starboard motor, so I'll be putting down in Cleveland for approximately forty-five minutes."

If you don't believe me, ask Perry Lafferty, senior vice-president of NBC. He was there. He swears it happened, and he's not one given to flights of fancy.

I had the pleasure of telling that story at Captain Morton's retirement dinner. A year later, flying his own single motor plane, he was making a landing on a tiny airstrip in his own backyard when a fuel line broke, totally obscuring his vision. It's a long way from the hedgerows of Normandy to the wrong side of Florida.

(TAPES CLICK OFF)

They kept at me, those doctors. "Try going to your office. Go, if only for a few hours."

The office? I went. A dusty cave of memories. I had nothing to do there, just five minutes of bullshitting with the janitor and checking my ancient mail. Not much, just a threat from the phone company attached to a virgin bill. "Unless you make some calls, you will be presumed to be dead or missing."

"Well, fuck you, Ma Bell. I bailed out over Burbank. I'll make phone calls again! I'll come back!" Oh, how I wanted to come back! Why was it taking so long? It's true that I looked better. My weight was up to normal. I had some surprisingly good days; and also some devastating setbacks. But when would it finally leave me? A friend of mine had a five-bypass operation in a faraway place (whisked there in Frank Sinatra's Lear jet). A few weeks later he was on the Carson show getting screams with a lot of inside stories about angiograms and bedpans. Why couldn't I do that? *My* illness was just as hilarious as his!

I did do one show, a TV interview with a marvelous man named Tom Cottle. I went expecting the usual pap questions, only to discover that Tom Cottle is a practicing psychiatrist from Boston, with all the tricks of the analytical trade. He proceeded to strip me wide open in front of his millions of viewers. At one point, I wept. The mail that followed was a deluge of letters that asked for nothing—no autographs, no pictures, nothing. Just hundreds and hundreds of caring people wanting me to know that they had *heard* me, and they understood what I was going through. They cared and wanted to share their love.

One very sincere gentleman sent me a book he had written in which he claimed that earth had a secret population that came from outer space. With it was a note that said it was highly likely that I was from another planet, and what I was suffering from was really a giant, astro, jet lag.

But the rest of the letters made sense, and they all said that I was in their prayers. These were strangers! I couldn't get over it, they cared about me and were praying for me!

"Get out your little white gloves and your hat, Henny, we're going to church!"

I remember it was a Wednesday morning when I read the article. It was about a hypnotherapist billed modestly as "Healer to the Stars." It went on to tell of some of his amazing exploits: restoring the voice of one of the world's greatest pop singers; getting a booze-ridden pitcher out of the rubber sheets long enough to hurl a World Series no-hitter; bestowing unusual sexual powers on a young President.

An hour later, I was in the guru's office. I must say, he was impressive. He had penetrating eyes, a mellifluous voice, and was beautifully clad in a suit by Giorgio's. On his feet were a pair of humble Gucci loafers bearing the insignia of The Fisherman, a gift from a grateful Pope.

After a pre-treatment conference in which I told him of the evaluation of the whiz kids, the doctor said, "I know them. They're shmucks! All doctors are shmucks! Ignore them. Just lie back and relax. Listen to me, and go to sleep. Just relax."

He then proceeded to put me under by swinging a Fabergé amulet before my eyes.

"You are now in a deep sleep . . . sleep . . . sleep! You do not have Parkinson's or any other disease. You can walk . . . walk . . . now . . . get up and walk!"

To my amazement, I got up and I walked. I walked around his spacious office. Still intoning, he opened the door to a long hall and ordered me to walk the length of it, swinging his glorious amulet as I went.

"Now, hear me good," he crooned, "All doctors are full of shit! You can walk! Parkinson's, my ass! Now, run! Run like O. J. Simpson in that commercial. No, wait a minute! First, give me the check. Good! Now, get going!"

I took off like a scalded dog.

"Turn left for the elevators. Wait! This is your mantra. Let's hear it: 'All doctors are full of shit!'" Three somber gentlemen in golf togs dropped their little black bags in stunned indignation.

Soon I was out in the street. Using my posthypnotic suggestion, I rapped three times on a parking meter and came to, fully awake and feeling god-awful. I started to get into my car and, as usual, tripped over my own feet. So much for hypnotic healing.

I then tried another kind of cure. I found a lady psychonutritionist who put me on a diet of only one food: saltless vegetable broth with a kelp float. She arrived at this by looking deep into my eyes and feeling my glands for a good twenty minutes. Oh, *great!* I lost eleven pounds in five days; then Henny rescued me with a steak.

You get pretty desperate when you are sick for so long. I even tried the "laying on of hands." The healer didn't actually touch me. He just waved his hands over my head while chanting something in an unknown tongue. So help me, I felt a great surge of heat.

"Walk," he commanded.

I did. As a matter of fact, I ran. A brushfire in your toupé is hardly conducive to dawdling.

Well, so much for the miracle cures. Besides, what was a layer-on-of-hands, a speaker in tongues, doing living in a condominium? All right, maybe a cave, but at the very most a vacant store. (Did you hear about the wealthy gypsy who owned a chain of empty A&Ps?) I guess when it comes to miracle cures, I'm of the old school. I want a conical hat, a seething cauldron, some powdered unicorn horn, and fillet of salamander.

"Double, double toil and trouble."

So, back to the veranda and my padded chair. My head is bending low. "Fetch me a mint julip, Miss Henny, while I dream of days gone by."

"Do the crosstown buses run all night?"

"Doodah, Doodah!" *(Distant cannon)*

"Pardon me, Miss, do you keep stationary?"

"I do till the last minute, then I go crazy!" *(Muffled drum roll)*

"How do you get to Carnegie Hall?"

"Practice, my boy, practice!" *(Tom-toms)*

"Ah, yes, the natives are restless tonight."

18

It's a Wrap!

"IT'S A WRAP!" is an expression used in the film and television industry that is akin to "Taps" in the Army or "Auld Lang Syne" to all of us ringing in the new year.

At the end of a shooting day, when all the work that can be done has been done, the assistant director picks up his bullhorn and loudly proclaims, "It's a wrap!" This is a signal for mass good-byes, hugging and kissing, and after that, as far as I was concerned, a quick exodus from the set. For me, it always meant a fast drink with the cast and crew and get on home. I can still hear those Porsches double-clutching out the gate. In a little while, a needle in the local power station would flirt dangerously with "overload," as hundreds of our Jacuzzis, not to mention blenders, would be switched on.

Three years ago, when we started to write this book, the words literally spurted out. Good or bad, the experience was new and vibrant and ominous as it was, it cried to be written. Now the closing. How to say good-bye? It's a little like doing an act. The toughest part is the finish. How do you get off?

The first line in chapter one is, "Well, it looks like it might be Parkinson's disease." It would be so neat if those same two characters would hold aloft a fading sheaf of papers and cry, "We got it wrong! The patient doesn't have Parkinson's at all! It's just a virus."

If the book seems uneven, it's because I had to put it aside for weeks at a time. I was checked constantly by the doctors, and my symptoms would change. How could I convey what was happening when sometimes I had no idea myself; incidentally, nor did they.

When I told my agent that I was going to write a humorous book about a catastrophic disease, he was ecstatic.

"Can't miss," he said happily.

When I sent him the first few chapters, he was delirious.

"It's dynamite," he told me. "Let me have the whole thing as soon as you can. I can hardly wait for the last chapter, where you're cured."

"But I'm not going to be, if I really have Parkinson's," I answered. "Arrested maybe, contained perhaps. But I can't be cured."

He was suddenly catatonic. "But how?" he exploded. "How are you going to make the 'Chicken-a-la-king' circuit? You gotta be cured!"

I knew what that meant. Henny and I had written two books, so we had been forced to do the "chicken-a-la-king" circuit ourselves. Not only once, but twice.

The "chicken-a-la-king" circuit is a tour of ten to fifteen cities and consists of radio and TV appearances, book-signing parties, generally staged in bookshops and department store windows and, most of all, at luncheons, where the author gets up and speaks. It's grueling, and if you are a smash you get to do the same thing in England and Australia. But, if you want to be an author nowadays you'd better be prepared to tour, and you'd better be in very good health.

As we remembered those tours, the hotel rooms, the restaurants, the department stores, and the bookshops all changed, but the cast of authors remained the same. I imagine it was a lot like it must have been years ago playing vaudeville. There we sat day after day, the same authors smiling at each other over mountains of cantaloupe balls, rivers of consommé, glaciers of tomato aspic, and those little patties that soon seemed like tiny volcanos, as they erupted their molten chicken lava. After the endless luncheons, still smiling at each other, we got up and made our speeches. We all knew each other's talks by heart. I'm sure they got as sick of ours as we did of theirs.

One book that didn't quite make it, but that we never forgot was called *Where is Europe?*, a brilliant exposé of the unprincipled methods of mapmakers the world over. Another one that didn't do so well, entitled

Organ Exercises for Four hands, was really a very valuable book for those who were lucky enough to have four hands, or even four organs.

So, I continued to write this book. But forced to write in spurts and unable to act, I tried to think of other things to channel my teeming mind. Produce! That was it! I'd produce a movie! By now, I certainly must have absorbed the producing know-how by osmosis. "I'll find a script," I told Henny. "I'll send out feelers. Chum the Hollywood waters."

I did, and I got a nibble right away. A young writer with fairly good credits showed up. He had a new "treatment." Virgin territory. "Good," I thought, "now I could be the head of the venture right from my fire-lit lair, without moving from my special chair with the needlepoint-covered, rubber doughnut."

Nancy ushered in the young man. We exchanged amenities and the current story, the one about the pig with the wooden leg. I looked him over. "Great!" Iron-gray untrimmed crew cut, over-sized shades, a corduroy jacket with leather elbows, unpressed canvas slacks topping white sweat socks and blue-and-red jogging shoes. "He had to be talented!" Through the window I could see his car, a battered, topless MG, with English license plates and those little sports car medals. "Another Paddy Chayefsky!," I told myself. As he made himself comfortable, he looked around the room and out into the garden. "This must be the old Herbert Marshall house."*

An unsung genius, that's what he was!

I noticed he sounded like William F. Buckley, with just the correct number of "Oy vay's," "schlepping's," and "yenta's" larding his conversation. "Odets and Cheever in one package!," I murmured to myself. He started to outline his screenplay, using the words "dichotomy" and "protaganist." "Marvelous! This is a mensch," I thought. "I'll go right to the bank! Unlimited financing, that's what I'll get!"

"To put it in a nutshell," he explained, "this story is unlike anything I've ever done. It's a whole new approach. You'll love it! It's about cancer!"

I was stunned. "Cancer!" I was so shocked, I almost made it out of my

---

*Herbert Marshall house: In Hollywood, a house is always referred to by the name of its most famous previous owner. Thus, when you get directions from someone, it's apt to be, "Turn left at the old Garbo house, then make a right at the old Taylor-and-Stanwyck place." This will never be referred to as the "Backus house" until long after we are gone.

chair my myself. "Why in God's name would you want to write about that?" Words failed me. "It's, it's," I sputtered, "it's such a depressing subject. People want to see movies about happy, uplifting things, not cancer!!"

"You don't understand," he replied. "It's a musical."

On the way out he patted Nancy's tusch.

Gradually, after much prodding, I began getting out of the house, sometimes with disastrous results. Partway through dinner my legs would cramp, causing such pain that I would waffle on the brink of consciousness. At times, my lower body would lock, and it would take two waiters with warm spoons* to pry me out of the banquette.

At other times, roving charley horses would ravage my torso like a demented fire-eater snapping at a crepe suzette.

Fall down. Get up. Fall down. Get up. "Get back on the horse!" I'd make myself return to the same restaurants. Once, I even made it past the entrance. A week later, I got all the way into the banquette. Another time, through the salad. Then one night, it happened! I made it through the antipasto! Then the pasta, which I twirled with the touch of a blacksmith. Then the salad. And now, the chocolate mousse. ("Mommy, mommy, there's a moose in my room!" "Well, eat it, darling, before it melts!") I was reeling. Almost there. A cup of coffee and a pony of brandy. I made it! I made it!

Adventures in graceful dining. My poor Henny.

THIS IS HENNY

My poor Jimmy. Not once in these four years was he comfortable. And the strange variety of pains!

"Help me, Henny. I can't eat. My spoon fell. My hands won't work!"

"Help me, Henny. I can't get into the bed."

He couldn't climb in, or slide up or down, or turn over, or even sit up, without being hoisted—and all night long, to the bathroom with all of that, and back to bed, hoisted.

Warm Spoon: an apocryphal tale of a young apprentice who was trying out for a job at Maxim's. He was under the eye of the maitre d' while serving an amply endowed beauty. Suddenly one of her breasts popped out of her décolletage. Without missing a beat, the deft apprentice backhanded the diner's boob back into her bodice. When he returned to his station the all-seeing Maitre d' said, "Well done, mon fils, but at Maxim's we use a warm spoon."

"Sleep, my darling. Forget the pain. Try to be comfortable."

And the showers. He complained that he never felt really clean. The bathtub was out. So was the pool. He couldn't swim or dive anymore, and the steps were steep and bannisterless. A shower? How? Well, it had to be in tandem. How do you hold up a man, soap him, rinse him, and keep both of you from slipping? How do you get him and yourself out of there? Soon the whole bathroom was a shower. There was so much water in there that one day we saw a rainbow.

"Don't worry, Jimmy darling, as soon as I dry you and get you back into bed, I'll make you spaghetti and a sundae."

It was hard enough for him to manage pasta at the table, let alone in bed. The place was a shambles. Time for another shower. Spaghetti all over. But you've got to give him credit. He did it without a net!

"Dress me, Henny, I can't."

"Drive me, Henny, I can't."

"My teeth hurt. I can't talk. I'll never be able to act again if I can't talk!"

"I'll take you to the dentist."

"I can't work on him, Henny, he's too sick."

All day long, "I can't!"—"I can't!"—"I can't!"

And the doctors told me, "He's got the 'I can'ts' again. Stop pampering him. The only way to stop it is to make him take charge of his own life. Turn a deaf ear, Henny!"

I tried.

"You're looking great, Henny. How do you do it?"

How did I? Was I enjoying this? Was I simply delighted because I had him all to myself? Was it because I felt so useful? Whatever! What difference did it make? I never for one moment let the thought that he would *not* get well enter my mind. He had to! And I had to work at it to make it happen. Anyway, I'd rather be with Jimmy sick, than with any other person on earth. I never get tired of him. They tell us that without health there is nothing, but what do they speak of love?

THIS IS JIM

I feel a little better. The Nardils work. My depression lifted.

One thing the medical troika agreed on, "Get his ass out of there! See people. Go to the theater." I went twice. Once to the Ahmanson and once to the Shubert. Both theaters have that new innovation: no aisles. Once you're in, you're in. The architects really went out of their way to disguise the fact that these are theaters. Had John Wilkes Booth tried his tricks here, he would have ended up in the Sushi Bar. In these horrendous hangers, the stage is two light-years away from the audience, and as for the balconies, forget it! They are in yet another time warp. The acoustics are totally nonexistent and the stages are badly "miked," causing the cast to sound like tobacco auctioneers.

Backstage, it's even worse. The Ahmanson, for one, has all the clinical charm of the County General Hospital. No lovable old geezer called "Pop" is at the stage door, doling out mail and dressing room keys. Instead, there's a uniformed civil servant with side arms. The dressing rooms have all the ambiance of hot-bed motel rooms. No call boy clangs his way up the iron stairway to your door to call out, "Places, please!" Instead, you hear a voice over closed circuit TV. Big brother is indeed watching!

The stage itself is as deserted and barren as the dark side of the moon. No ropes, no flats, and the curtains are automated. The whole thing is controlled by the stage manager punching little buttons. (His own private space probe.) Gone are the crusty old stagehands playing pocket pool. When you stand on one of these stages ready to make your entrance, you are alone—you, your Maker, and the IBM. I should know. I was there. Mr. Ahmanson and Mr. Shubert, a plague on both your houses!

THIS IS HENNY

Well, the nightmare is almost over, and so is this book. Just think, the Parkinson's disease, the prostate, the paralysis, the panic, the depression—all that confusing horror that could have been cut in half, had it not been for the misevaluation.

It took two years for them to decide to take him off L-Dopa, to see how he would respond. After six months, when he started to improve without it, he was *still* convinced that he really had Parkinson's and that we were all lying to him. Or that he had something worse that we were keeping from him. He had every right to be frightened and suspicious. He had had so many confusing "opinions" that he was pulled every which way. How could he allow himself to accept the fact that there was nothing organically wrong with him—that his was a stress-induced psychosomatic illness that only he himself could cure?

He had every right to take it out on me, to take it out on his doctors, to take it out on the world! He became so panic-ridden that often it would rub off on me, and then, for a short time, I would become one of the millions of Americans who, like Jim, suffer from it. Fortunately, I had lots of help from all the expected places: friends and family; our dear Doctor Rick; Jim's two supportive analysts, Tony and R.G.; and, of course, those many, many fans who wrote and sent their love. I was able to lean on them and on the beautiful AA prayer:

> God grant me the serenity to accept
> the things I cannot change,
> the courage to change the things I can,
> and the wisdom to know the difference.

Good-bye, and thanks to all of you.

And now the wind is at our back, and it's shady all the way.

THIS IS JIM

My life had been rushing to a crescendo. Maybe the crisis was a good thing, a chance to pause, take stock, look around. I remember playing golf with the great and colorful Jimmy Demaret on his own course in Houston. As we were walking along the fairway, he stopped, looked around, took a deep breath and said, "You know, Jim, I've been playing golf for almost fifty years, walking around in these beautiful parks, and I'm just beginning to take time to smell the flowers." Now, some years later, I finally realize what he meant.

Henny has one of the loveliest gardens in town. Did I know that? Did I realize that our terrace is covered with pot after pot of orchids? It's alive with wrist corsages, and I never even noticed. She took a course in African violets culture. They even named a variety after her, "The Henny Bakus." The house is full of them. Big purple things, but I paid no attention. She said, "Look at them, Jimmy, they're beautiful! Talk to them." So I tried, but I gave it up when one of her African violets called me a 'Honky.'"

"Take a negative and turn it into a positive," they said. I kept trying, but it's so hard to do. It must work. It's in all the books. Medical books, spiritual books, philosophy books—all of them. And the message is loud and clear. Take a handicap and make it work *for* you. Why was it so hard for me? Actors do it all the time. In a performance, when something goes wrong, we are taught to "use it!" It's one of the first things you learn. "Use it!" I couldn't even do that with the most inconsequential things. For example, it occurred to me that I hadn't bought any new clothes in

121

more than three years. I went into one of my panics. Wait a minute! What was I panicked about? Where was I going? So my suits weren't new, so the lapels were an eighth of an inch off. Who would notice? George Hamilton? The clothing industry would survive. They would survive even if I slapped a red gumdrop in the middle of my forehead, slipped into a diaper, and started to weave myself a "44 long." Besides, what do clothes mean, anyway? Once, I was lousy with suits and what did it mean? Not a thing! Good! My panic eased.

When I was shooting "I Married Joan" they made me one or two suits for every show. I wore thirty to forty suits a season that the tailors were happy to make in return for the credit at the end of the show:

MR. BACKUS'S WARDROBE BY HOUSE OF WORSTED TEX

When we went off the air for good, the production company gave them to me, all of them! So, after a four-year run, I was an unemployed actor with a basement full of suits.

I kept giving them away. I had the only gardener in Bel-Air who trimmed hedges in a tux. Sometimes in an emergency, in lieu of cash, I would tip the delivery boy with one. "Care for something in a herring bone?"

I was also practicing to never look back. "Don't look back; they may be gaining on you," was the sage advice from Satchel Paige, the venerable, black ballplayer, whose actual age and foot size were never established. (Little known fact: When he took a shower, the fact that he couldn't close the door lends credence to the "feet" legend, doesn't it?) I started to look forward. I was on my way.

"Keep at it, Jim," the doctors told me. "It may not be Parkinson's, after all. Remember what we told you? Parkinson's cannot be diagnosed, only evaluated, and you *are* getting well." Well? From what?

So, to put my hypochondriacal mind at ease, the Boys of Autumn whisked me over to the UCLA Medical Center, where I once again heard that ambiguous word, "evaluation." This time, at UCLA, and from their head boy.

The UCLA Medical Center has more treadmills, whirlpools, and tinker toys that light up, than Magic Mountain. Their Neurological Center, I understand, makes Mayo's look like a Christian Science reading room. Incidentally, if you buy the five hundred dollar evaluation ticket, you get to go on all the rides.

Once again, two strange words were aired: *basal ganglion.* That's what they all finally and, at long last, agreed upon. So guess what? I have a basal ganglion. I really do! It seems a basal ganglion sometimes mimics Parkinson's disease. As near as I can make out, I have a crossed circuit between my brain and my limbs. I have this, in addition to my loose hardware. Oh great! Okay, fellas, "Communications down!" . . . "Faulty wiring!" . . . Ma Bell would never put up with this! For example, my brain will say, "Right foot, step out!"

Right foot to brain, "Bugger off!"

As for the left foot, "Up yours, brain!"

I predict that the basal ganglion will be to the 80s what whiplash was to the 50s, what hepatitis was to the 60s, and what hiatus hernia was to the 70s. So, I'm gonna flaunt it, baby! There's a light shining at the end of the cornucopia. As for you doctors, "Who loves ya, baby?"

But remember this. Wherever some poor mother of three is kept waiting an hour, while the doctor recounts his golf game to his latest bimbo, I'll be there! Wherever some poor working stiff forks over fifty dollars from his Christmas Club for an office visit and then is told, "We don't validate," I'll be there! Wherever some poor guy calling from an open pay phone in the pouring rain with his last dime is then put on hold, I'll be there! I'll be there, lurking in the darkness, but I'll be there!

Well, I'm plugging on. I *am* trying, and it is working, and except for a few odds and ends, it's time to get off. Henny said, "Jimmy, you're on too long. You're like that ex-husband of Jane Wyman's. Remember what she said about him? Don't ask him what time it is, or he'll tell you how to make a watch!" So, I guess I'll take Henny's advice, and, as they say on Madison Avenue, "I'll put a ribbon on it, button it, and head for the barn."

We take for granted every simple bodily function. Walking is one of them. And here I was, thanks to the basal ganglion and my dim bulb, faced with the task of learning how to do it all over again. I thought about that. "Okay, if I have to learn once again," I thought, "why do it the way I used to? Improve it!" Good idea. So I tried to visualize walks I had admired. Marilyn Monroe and her famous sexy glide, which she told me she developed by imitating Robert Mitchum, who stole it from John Wayne! Think about it. Jack Benny? That was a great walk. Think about that for a minute. It was slightly effeminate perhaps, but as George Burns once said, "Put a nice dress on Jack, and you can take him anywhere." Another lovely walk is that of the energetic and graceful

Juliet Prowse doing her panty hose commercial. And how about those African tribes gliding about the veldt with those loads on their heads? So now I'm trying to imitate a ballerina played by John Wayne delivering a CARE package to Albert Schweitzer. "Have head, will travel"!

Walking was one thing. How about dancing? I used to dance. Now that I was walking pretty well, it was time to dance again. I tried, but my feet were glued to the floor. So, again, I panicked! My panic was followed by a segue into a chorus of "Used to Be." And then I remembered something wonderful that R.G. told me sometime back. He said, "Do the best you can with what you've got."

Do the best you can with what you've got! Great! So I enrolled in a ballet class. This was getting down to basics. I've been working very hard at it. The ballet master assures me that I'm making progress. "You're doing very well at the barre!" he told me. Yeah, sure. I'm afraid that's the story of my life.

My sister-in-law, Florence, with the B.A., the Ph.D., the B.M., the B.C., the B.S. (the letters after her name look like an eye chart), sent me an article about Eugene O'Neill, a complex man to put it mildly. He spent the last years of his life convinced (and by doctors, mind you) that he was suffering from Parkinson's disease. He had all the classic symptoms, head shaking, tremors, shuffling gait, the staggers, all of them. Later he found out that it wasn't Parkinson's at all. It was a twenty-five-year-old hangover!!

Bottoms up, Mr. O'Neill. Maybe I should have called this book *Mourning Becomes Electra*. So, here I am, a little older than I used to be, having to learn how to walk, move, sing, and dance—everything all over again.

This time I'm going to get it right!!

"Henny, what if they made another mistake and I really do have Parkinson's? What'll I do?"

"Write a sequel."